"Building an enterprise from the earliest stages to maturity requires more art than science, and this book provides wonderful personal insights into many of the decisions and stages a leader faces along the way."

LARRY SONSINI
Chairman, Wilson Sonsini Goodrich & Rosati
Chairman, Commission on Corporate Governance,
New York Stock Exchange

"These chapters should be re-packaged in envelopes, so that when you open each letter you can read it slowly, thoughtfully, even more than once, and savor the insights. Few authors, business executives, or entrepreneurs have been willing, as Levy has, to let us into their heads and inside their hearts, telling us not only what to think about, what feelings we'll need to come to grips with, but most importantly why any of this matters in building meaningful relationships and institutions. Herein is Levy's legacy, meant to provide guidelines to the next generation of entrepreneurs and others who aspire to make a difference."

BARRY Z. POSNER, PhD
Professor of Leadership and former Dean, Santa Clara
    University
Coauthor of *The Leadership Challenge* and *The Truth
    about Leadership*

"These are thoughtful, insightful letters that every entrepreneur should read. Building a company is an immensely difficult task that too many embark on blindly. These letters provide marvelous insight into the very personal, very human elements that an entrepreneur should understand."

GIB MYERS
Partner Emeritus, Mayfield Fund
Founder and Director, Entrepreneurs Foundation
Co-founder, Center for Social Innovation, Stanford
    Graduate School of Business

"*Letters to a Young Entrepreneur* is truly fabulous ... a real 'love story,' but with 'feet on the ground' sensitivities regarding an entrepreneur's personal journey."

> JAMES L. KOCH
> Director, Global Social Benefit Incubator
> School of Business Administration, Santa
>   Clara University

"This collection of 'letters' takes me back to the delightful *Tuesdays with Morrie* but with a successful entrepreneur, Ricardo Levy. Maybe *Mondays with Ricardo* would have been another title. For over three years I have been the beneficiary of Ricardo's insight and wisdom, honed over decades of real entrepreneurship on the ground. From absorbing uncertainty to controlling hubris and from spiritual quiet time to layoffs and building a wonderful board of directors, this book has it all. He speaks of companions we meet along the way, and I certainly regard him as one of the rare and wonderful such individuals that too seldom enter one's life."

> ROBERT WORSLEY
> Founder, Skymall Inc.
> Chairman and CEO, Renegy Holdings, Inc.

"What a marvelous meeting of faces here—faces that do not always meet! Ricardo Levy has put together the very practical with the possible and the profound. If you want to do many and good things, and do them at a higher level, I would encourage you to read this fine and inspiring book."

> FATHER RICHARD ROHR
> Founding Director, Center for Action and Contemplation,
>   Albuquerque, NM
> Author of *Simplicity: The Freedom of Letting Go*

LETTERS TO A YOUNG ENTREPRENEUR

LETTERS TO A YOUNG ENTREPRENEUR

Ricardo B. Levy

CATALYTIC PUBLISHERS

San Francisco · Honolulu · Prague

Cover and text design by David Bullen Design.

For further information or discussion about the ideas in this book,
please write to RicardoLevy@me.com or visit www.RicardoLevy.com.

ISBN 978-1-4515-5840-1

To Noella,
my treasured companion

Contents

$\mathcal{I}$NTRODUCTION

My motivation in writing *Letters to a Young Entrepreneur* is to share with you some of my own experiences during a three-decade journey in business leadership. My emphasis is less on specific business issues or detailed solutions to problems and more on the "inner world of an entrepreneur," the person who sometimes struggles to cope with the many fascinating—and at times difficult—situations confronted in building a business.

I have a confession to make: I am biased. I believe that nothing is more exciting than starting and building companies. I feel this way even after realizing that my greatest business successes occurred in areas where I did not anticipate them, and my greatest failures in situations where I thought that the enterprise had it made. That is humbling. But it does not take away the great pride that comes with being a key driver, the profound feeling that I made a difference in many people's lives and created value for both investors and society.

The entrepreneurial spirit was ingrained in me in my youth. When I was a small boy, surrounded by three different businesses, I would wake up every morning (including Saturdays) at 7:00 AM to the sounds of my father preparing to open the doors to the bristle and paintbrush factory building at the back of our house to admit the hundred or so employees who worked for him. My mother would prepare breakfast for me, get me ready for school, and then go to another part of the back building to prepare the ingredients to make cosmetics. My brother—sixteen years older than I—would already be in his laboratory, testing new ways of extracting natural products for making insecticides that were safe for humans. So, as I pedaled my bicycle to school at 8:30, my home was already buzzing with commercial activity.

This was the early 1950s in Quito, Ecuador—the daily life for a family of Jewish immigrants who had escaped from Germany in the early 1940s to one of the few countries that would accept them when the Nazis were sweeping through Europe. Many of our peers followed the same path, finding ways of using their commercial and manufacturing skills to survive. Some, like my father, had brought their trade from the old country. Others, like my mother, acquired a new trade rather late in life. She was then thirty-five and a housewife. Shortly before they left Europe, she learned from a local chemist to make lipstick, shampoo, and hand lotion in the family garage, knowing that this skill would help the family survive in a new country. Or like my brother, who applied an interest in science that had flourished since his childhood to the discovery of new applications for natural products that were unique to their host country.

I was a latecomer in this family. My brother, Werner Ludwig, was born in 1929 in the small town of Kaiserslautern, near Frankfurt. Shortly after his son's birth, my father had an intuition about what was brewing in Europe and decided not to have more children until the political climate was better defined. His insight proved visionary. With his deep interest in law, he witnessed all the judges who did not belong to the Nationalist Socialist Party being dismissed and replaced with party members when Hitler was named chancellor in 1933. He realized that this was the beginning of the end and warned the rest of the family of the imminent danger. He urged all of them to get out of Germany.

Getting out was very difficult to contemplate. The family traced its German roots back to the twelfth century. Its members could not comprehend that they had to abandon this beautiful land that had been their home for so many centuries. They did not wish to leave. Yet my father was persistent and left with my mother and four-year-old brother, going to nearby Switzerland to stay close enough to help the other relatives if the need arose. Being a born inventor, he was able to establish himself quickly on the basis of one of his patents: the first reusable toothbrush that did not lose bristles when it was boiled to disinfect it. He set up a small company to manufacture these toothbrushes, earning a reasonable income. In 1938, when the situation for Jews in Germany became really dire, he managed to bring the rest of the family members out.

In 1940 my father led my four grandparents, my mother, and my brother on a five-month odyssey—first overland to Lisbon, and then by ship to America. He also helped another part of the family escape via Siberia and Japan. Unable to enter the United States, both groups went to Ecuador, a country of high mountains and raging rivers, with a different language and different customs, but nevertheless a land of freedom. I was born five years later.

The entrepreneurial spirit was their means of survival in this new land. Soon after arriving in the capital, Quito, at the foot of the majestic snow-covered Andean mountains, my parents bought some land on the outskirts of the city to build a house. It was on a dirt road, but they figured that the city would come to them, and the property's value would increase. They built a second house in the back, a two-story building designed to be a two-apartment unit, but with no interior walls (much like a loft or a basement that is finished later). The open space would serve as the site for the family businesses. The fallback would be to convert the building into rental property if necessary. Twenty-five years later, after my father died, this rental property provided the main financial sustenance for my mother.

The entrepreneurial spirit was in my brother as well. He was very interested in extracting the large variety of natural products that grew in Ecuador's diverse climate regions. In 1949, after reading an article in *Time* magazine about a professor in the United States who was studying such plants, he came to Stanford University to study with him. He had just turned twenty. Four years later he received a PhD in biochemistry and returned to Ecuador to expand his young natural products business. His primary interest was in a plant that produced an insecticide that was harmless to warm-blooded animals: pyrethrum. He developed an efficient extraction method at his manufacturing plant, which he still runs at the age of eighty. Pyrethrum and its synthetic counterparts have since become the key ingredients in most safe household insecticides.

The rhythm of the family's life was very European. While we were not very religious, our family values were deep and ever present. We had a sense of gratitude and awe—and a sense of insatiable curiosity. My grandfather, by then in his eighties, would sit at the head of the table with a large encyclopedia on a stand by his side, ready to be consulted when the conversation turned to a subject that needed elucidation. My mother would use Latin and Greek phrases when the occasion called for them, and many are still imprinted in my mind: *"si tacuisses, philosophus mansisses"* (if you had kept your mouth shut, you would have remained a philosopher); or *"de gustibus non est disputandum"* (you cannot argue about tastes). Curiosity and gratitude, and my mother's wisdom, have accompanied me throughout my life. I once asked her what she felt when she came to this foreign land not even knowing the language. She answered very simply: "I looked up at the blue sky and saw freedom." She lived for the rest of her life in Ecuador and died at the age of ninety-seven in 2002.

Recently, my good friend Glenda Burgess wrote in *The Geography of Love:* "what you dream of yourself at fourteen reflects your purest wish."[1] At fourteen, my life was fully immersed in the comings and goings of my refugee family.

Business was everywhere in our household. I overheard the lunch and dinner conversations on whom to hire and whom to fire, what to call a new product and what product was not making it, what the competition was doing and how to enter the export business. I sensed the obstacles and observed how they were resolved. Most important, I saw an unswerving sense of optimism. Never did I hear "this cannot be done" or "we need to give up." The glass was always at least half full. Gratitude for life and freedom was in the air. My father was a dominating figure, but I never heard him raise his voice. He was stubborn and demanding, sometimes to a frustrating degree for a teenager, yet never was there any question about his love and his motives. His family came first.

As I finished high school in 1962, two things were clear to me: I was going to go to college in the United States, and afterward I was going to return to Ecuador. I had my heart set on Stanford University, influenced by both my brother and his wife, Traute, who was one of the first female graduates of the civil engineering department at Stanford. Since graduating, she has been a steadfast co-journeyer on my brother's entrepreneurial path. I also knew "in my blood" that when I finished college I would go into business for myself, imagining that I would follow in the footsteps of my parents and my brother.

But destiny had its own plans: I fell in love with an American woman, and I fell in love with science. Interestingly, it was the science that eventually anchored me in the United

States. My wife, Noella, would have followed me to my foreign homeland if that had been my decision. In fact, we did return to Ecuador for a brief period right after we married; my father had passed away, and I had to help run the family businesses. However, the pull of science was too strong. I sold the businesses and came back to Stanford to complete my PhD.

For my studies I picked a very practical subject: catalysis. Most products we consume, from gasoline to margarine, undergo a catalytic step somewhere in their manufacture. In fact, catalysis is so ubiquitous that life itself could not exist without the continuous action of the most sophisticated of catalysts: enzymes. So, even in my choice of scientific work I gravitated to a topic that would once again immerse me in business. In 1974, after working for two years at Exxon, I was inspired to start my own company, Catalytica, with my PhD adviser and mentor, Michel Boudart, and with Jim Cusumano, a good friend, technical colleague, and executive at Exxon. Our dream was to use our scientific knowledge to create more effective and environmentally friendly manufacturing processes. We were frustrated with the inefficiency of existing approaches, and we knew we could do better. We also knew that other scientists and engineers would welcome the opportunity to work in an environment of minimum bureaucracy and red tape.

Initially we started a contract research organization in 1974. In the early '80s, we transformed it to focus solely on the discovery of novel chemical systems. By the early '90s we had used our extensive patent estate to start three different companies.

One, in the pharmaceutical industry, became very successful and was eventually sold to a European conglomerate in 2000, after reaching sales of over $500 million and a market capitalization of almost $1 billion. Another, in the energy industry, was a technological success but a market failure—it was ahead of its time. That company morphed several times and is now a renewable-energy company. And a third business, in the computational field, is still a small software company making its mark in specialized areas that require fast, complex data analysis. It is private and is finding its "niche."

In *Letters to a Young Entrepreneur*, I describe some of the forces that determined my choices as we built these companies—and some factors that prevented me from taking paths that in retrospect I think I should have taken. When I speak about the inner drives that define the entrepreneur and the external qualities that make him or her a good leader, I am exploring the behavioral drivers that I felt and feel. When I talk about the covenant that a true entrepreneurial leader undertakes, I am talking about the sense of obligation that defined my own behavior. When I speak of the trust that the leader receives from people along on the journey, and how it helps some ease their sense of uncertainty, I am focusing on one of the key ingredients that helped me grow my businesses. And when I talk about the challenges of stepping down, I am sharing my inner struggle about moving on and letting others take over the baby that I had created.

So, this book is intended as a very personal sharing of my life as an entrepreneur in a way that I hope is useful to others who are engaged in the exciting and creative task of business building and who have made leadership their vocation. I am speaking to the entrepreneur who is forever young at heart, since the journey is by definition one of continuous renewal, discovery, and learning. My reward will come when the reader sees a concept that touches him or her and has a little "aha!" that makes life clearer and more fulfilling.

Enjoy.

Ricardo Levy

LETTERS TO
A YOUNG
ENTREPRENEUR

1

Inner Qualities of
an Entrepreneur

As you sit by yourself at a restaurant and sketch a great new idea on a napkin, wondering whether you have what it takes to pursue it by starting your own business, ask yourself three simple questions: Is your yearning for this new and different idea deep and irresistible? When you dream of the future, do you dream big and feel that your dream will benefit many? Can you see opportunity, rather than difficulty, in all challenges? If the answer to these is yes, you are ready.

To have passion, to have a dream, to have a purpose in life. And there are three components to that purpose, one is to find out who you really are, to discover God, the second is to serve other human beings, because we are here to do that, and the third is to express your unique talents, and when you are expressing your unique talents you lose track of time.

DEEPAK CHOPRA

Dear Entrepreneur:

O N A COLD MONDAY MORNING at Exxon, where I worked, I happened to overhear a conversation between Jim Cusumano and his technician that was to change both our lives. Jim, holding a report, said, "Joe, these test results look incredibly exciting, yet I doubt that the company will ever pay much attention. Our invention just will not fit Exxon's commercial revenue threshold. If we could only convince them to sell us the rights to this technology, we could create a very interesting—and different—company!"

A strange sense of excitement swept over me, the kind that made the hairs on the back of my neck stand up. I rushed over to Jim, pulled him into his office, and asked if he was serious—not about the invention but about creating a new company, going out on his own. In answer, Jim pulled out of his desk drawer some of the "entrepreneurial notes" he kept on slips of paper as he jotted down ideas for new businesses. This conversation in the winter of 1973 set in motion a sequence of events that defined our lives for the next several decades.

Jim and I had become good friends, both socially and professionally, but we had never talked much about our careers. As it turned out, we both had a deep yearning to attain more direct control over our ideas and inventions, a desire to see

5

them move as fast as possible to commercialization, and an impatience with unnecessary red tape and bureaucracy.

Was I crazy to ever consider leaving my good position and promising career at a well-respected Fortune 500 corporation? I was not really unhappy at Exxon, which had hired me at age twenty-seven as part of a group of scientists and engineers working on important problems in the energy field. The United States had just faced the first major oil crisis since the discovery of petroleum, and we knew that we had to change the way we produced energy. I had some good ideas and was being recognized and promoted. I also had a wife and two small children, and my life seemed complete. By all conventional measures I was "on my way."

Nevertheless, I had a "bug," a feeling of being unsettled, of something missing. I felt as if I were encased in a large glass sphere. I could see the horizon through the glass but knew that I could not reach it without following defined corporate pathways, slowly climbing a prescribed ladder. The amount of oxygen in the sphere was carefully parceled out, and the allotted flow was just not enough for me. A large corporate organization could not satisfy my ingrained yearning to create my own business.

What I was feeling was the irrepressible *entrepreneurial itch*, the need to step out of the zone of security and into the uncertain world of a new venture. Surprisingly, all the members of my family—in spite of their own entrepreneurial DNA—were less than enthusiastic. The only person, aside from my wife, who supported this seemingly unrealistic dream was a cousin of my mother's, a concentration camp survivor who had restarted her life in America and was a deep believer in taking your destiny in your hands when the opportunity arose.

All my life I had been easily turned on by ideas and blessed with an enormously positive attitude. Every issue was an opportunity rather than a problem, a chance to clarify, influence, and convince. A silver lining always leaped immediately into my mind. I would get particularly excited about natural phenomena and think of ways to influence them. My imagination was constantly triggered by new observations, whether mine or someone else's, and I'd quickly envision practical ramifications. Often, my excitement made me impatient with barriers that seemed unnecessary or restrictions that impeded my actions. In this respect, Jim and I were very similar. As he put it, "For me, there was a push-pull reaction. Playing corporate games, wasting time and money, and seeing others make what I thought were the wrong decisions stifled my integrity."

So, after that fateful morning, Jim and I explored how we could apply our skills to launch a company. At first, any idea was fair game. We even considered making a simple toy that Jim had seen on a recent trip to Rome: a corrugated tube that made sounds (music?) when twirled around. We called it the "whirly whistle." Our stupidity in getting involved with that concept soon became evident when we could not get anyone to manufacture it, even among the many plastics manufacturers in the Highway 22 corridor of New Jersey. Gradually we realized that we needed to focus our attention on what we were trained for: harnessing the power of catalytic chemistry to manufacture useful chemical compounds with minimal environmental damage. The more we tested our ideas with others, the more we became convinced. The potential of catalytic concepts ignited a fire and passion within us that started to drive all our waking hours and even penetrated our dreams. Within a few months we could not stand any more delay. We had reached the *entrepreneurial tipping point*: an irrepressible urge to make the dream a reality. We quit our jobs and plunged into the creation of Catalytica.

So, dear entrepreneur, when you are fired up by a new idea for a business but you wonder whether you are ready to make the leap, consider these three questions: Is your yearning deep and irresistible? Is your dream big enough to benefit many? Do you see opportunity in all challenges? If your answers are yes, yes, and yes, go for it! While answering yes does not guarantee that you will succeed, it is an essential start. Once you have made the internal commitment, you are ready to consider transforming your idea into a viable company.

Best of luck,

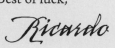

2

External Qualities of
an Entrepreneurial Leader

You need to become an engaging storyteller, one who conveys an authentic and convincing message, succeeds in infecting others with enthusiasm, and invites them to participate in the entrepreneurial dance. Most important, you need to be fully committed.

Until one is committed, there is hesitancy, the chance to draw back, always ineffectiveness. Concerning all acts of initiative (and creation), there is one elementary truth the ignorance of which kills countless ideas and splendid plans: that the moment one definitely commits oneself, then Providence moves too. A whole stream of events issues from the decision, raising in one's favor all manner of unforeseen incidents, meetings and material assistance, which no man could have dreamt would have come his way. I learned a deep respect for one of Goethe's couplets:

Whatever you can do or dream you can, begin it.
Boldness has genius, power and magic in it!

W. H. MURRAY

◊

Work like you don't need the money;
dance like no one is watching;
sing like no one is listening;
love like you've never been hurt;
and live life every day as if it were your last.

OLD IRISH PROVERB

Dear Entrepreneur:

*W*HEN YOU HAVE PASSED THE *entrepreneurial tipping point* and committed to your business dream, your work has only just begun. The list of tasks can be daunting, at times overwhelming—everything from building a team to assuring financing to defining your products. In this process, you have to channel both your innate and your developed skills. For me, those skills in their simplest form come down to telling a good story, moving with the flexibility and fluidity of a good dancer, and exuding an enthusiasm and genuineness that would make everyone fall in love with my dream. I call the roles that demand these skills the storyteller, the dancer, and the enthusiast. If you can do these well, you have a good chance.

The storyteller role may seem obvious on the surface—as I had assumed it was. Yet for me the real challenge of being an entrepreneur became conveying the message appropriately for the different audiences I had to address. I was used to communicating mainly to my technical colleagues, and, even though I prided myself on being able to simplify complex technical issues, not everyone was interested in the details, especially members of the financial community whom I was wooing to fund our company during the technology development phase.

My storytelling skill was tested most severely at Catalytica's first initial public offering (IPO). People called it a "road show," which I had always thought of as a performance tour by a music star. In many ways my show was no different. I was whisked from venue to venue in black stretch limos, flown to a different city in a whirlwind just about every day, and placed on a stage to give "the spiel." In my first appearance I was especially concerned about disappointing my sponsor, Fred Frank, the legendary and peripatetic dean of investment bankers (one of British Airways' and Air France's best Concord customers).

Much was riding on this IPO, including access to significant financing for the next critical phase of our company. I had practiced my talk intently, memorizing all my slides, until I could give the presentation mechanically. I knew that I would have only twenty minutes, so I tried to cram everything in by talking quickly. My effectiveness? When I finished there was silence, not one question, and I could see that everyone was eager to get out of the room and back to the daily task of trading stocks. My first show had been a dud.

Afterward, Fred took me aside and said simply, "Ric, too technical." I was so fascinated with the unique catalysts we had discovered that I failed to sense whether I was reaching the listener. I forgot the vital elements of communication: *connecting, conveying, and convincing.* I had failed in all three.

I never really *connected*; the financiers were there because Fred had asked them to come, not because they wanted to hear my story. When I *conveyed* my thoughts, I did not do so in language that they understood and with concepts that mattered to them. And without connecting and conveying I could hardly *convince* them that this company was one they needed to support—and buy. I had to make some changes, and quickly.

Back in my hotel room I spent the next twenty-four hours recrafting the presentation, making it much more personal, intimate, and relevant. It worked. The sixty presentations I made over the next three weeks went very differently. I was more engaged, more relaxed, and more confident. I interacted with the listeners rather than just presenting my side of the story, and I had a captive audience.

In the end we were able to take the company public. We succeeded in this critical mission, and a small but satisfying indicator was that I could open the *Wall Street Journal* and see our company listed. The enterprise had a chance to succeed.

Howard Gardner, in his book *Leading Minds*, speaks to the need for good storytelling.[2] He makes a convincing case that what distinguishes extraordinary leaders is the extent to which they both tell the story and, even more important, embody it. While Gardner's focus is on great scientific, political, and social leaders, such as Robert Oppenheimer,

George Marshall, Eleanor Roosevelt, Margaret Thatcher, and Martin Luther King Jr., his argument applies to entrepreneurs as well. We have to tell the story well and back it up by living it.

Ever since my first experience with the IPO road show, I have made a practice of mingling among my audience before a presentation. It gives me the pulse of the crowd and establishes one-on-one contact that serves as a link during the talk. It also allows me to adjust my words and my emphasis to what I've learned about the listeners, and it reminds me that communication is a very active give-and-take, much like a dance.

My Tai Chi teacher, Chungliang Al Huang, talks about a partner dance as a metaphor for the delicate and subtle interrelationships occurring in mentoring and leadership. This is how he described Tui Shou, or the Dance of Pushing Hands:

It is the dance between two willing and consenting partners, a dance of giving and receiving each other's gifts; a blending together in circular patterns as the hands surround the empty space between [the two] of them. Just as the empty space or hole in a cup, glass, or vase defines its function, so too the space or emptiness that exists between two people during the constant dance of pushing hands in Tai Ji is the essence of the relationship, the wisdom in the empty space between . . . partners.[3]

I have applied this dance metaphor to so many of my entrepreneurial dealings. It seems that every negotiation contains elements of Tui Shou, and many of my most serious conversations with employees can be characterized in the language of Chungliang, especially the attention I need to pay to the "empty space" between people as the place for reaching understanding and resolution.

I also found this to be true in our company's relationship with all major external constituents, including larger corporate partners. Partnering with large companies, an inevitable reality of most technology-based entrepreneurial companies (and many other new ventures), depends on developing good interpersonal contacts at multiple levels—from the highest decision maker to the working group. For the leader, a relationship with the top management is crucial. This relationship goes beyond company-to-company formality and establishes a one-on-one connection between individuals, a connection that is so necessary in any venture. It permits the real dance to take place.

Here's a good example. In 1993, Catalytica received an important investment from the large Japanese petrochemical company Mitsubishi Oil, one of that oil giant's first forays into funding an R & D company in the United States and a crucial endorsement of our efforts in the energy arena. I attribute the success of that relationship directly to the special connection Jim Cusumano and I developed with

Kikuo Yamada, Mitsubishi's CEO. We were introduced by Professor Kenzi Tamaru of Tokyo University, who knew our research well. Subsequently, Mr. Yamada took a personal interest in our entrepreneurial dream in the energy field. His direct involvement in our negotiations allowed us to cut through many complex issues, overcome communication and language difficulties, and complete the deal in record time, enabling us to showcase the Mitsubishi contract at our IPO. A measure of his sensitivity was that whenever we were with his team he made sure that nobody spoke Japanese, because we did not understand the language. It showed a very human and considerate dimension of this important leader.

The dance with Kikuo Yamada was not all business. We found many common personal interests. He loved music, both popular and classic. This dovetailed well with Jim Cusumano's past in the music business and my love of the symphony. I will never forget an evening when we hosted Mr. Yamada, his wife, and his entourage in San Francisco. To start the evening I had arranged for a string quartet from the San Francisco Symphony to play for us. That certainly set the mood. Then, during dinner, Mr. Yamada asked Jim to sing "Danny Boy"— *a cappella*. Mr. Yamada got so emotional that Mrs. Yamada pulled out a handkerchief and wiped his nose!

In 1994, Pfizer invested in our pharmaceutical subsidiary —one of the drug powerhouse's first investments in a small company not focused on drug discovery. That put our efforts in that field "on the map." It resulted directly from the close association we had developed with George Miln, president of Pfizer Research, and with Dan O'Shea, senior vice president of development.

Without O'Shea's personal comfort with us, such a relationship would not have been possible, because pharmaceutical companies always regarded manufacturing as their private and expert domain. It provided a foundation for our involvement in creating the manufacturing process for Aricept, which is now one of the major drugs for treating Alzheimer's disease.

Several years later, O'Shea provided his personal support and reference when we approached British-based Glaxo Wellcome, another pharmaceutical giant, with a proposal that we buy its flagship manufacturing facility in Greenville, North Carolina. I still remember the afternoon when Dan was on a speakerphone in a conference room at the Greenville plant with the senior Catalytica and Glaxo executives gathered to hear directly from one of our major customers. I could have floated out of the room on the praise that Dan volunteered about our quality and way of doing business. It helped convince the Glaxo group that the bet they were making on our small company was warranted.

One of the people in the room was Bob Ingram, then the head of Glaxo's U.S. operation and vice chairman of the British parent company. He was our internal champion, thanks to a personal introduction from Fred Frank and from one of our most important board members, Ernie Mario, who had previously served as CEO of Glaxo.[4] Bob extended his support throughout the difficult and long negotiations with Glaxo, and over the coming years I came to rely on him as a close adviser and ally, as our business with Glaxo grew to well over $400 million. No matter how busy he was— or in what part of the world he was traveling—he always took my call and listened to my issues. His personal contact was indispensable as I learned the subtleties of dealing with such a large customer, and he taught me never to hesitate to reach to the top of a company's management. Eventually Bob became CEO of the parent company and was stationed in London, but this never stopped him from being available to me and my company. His mentorship served me well in later years as we dealt with other large companies.

What caused these busy and successful leaders to pay attention to us—not just as a company but also as entrepreneurs? Beyond the potential of our innovations, I think it was that we embodied what many executives of large companies feel in the deep recesses of their minds: fascination with the entrepreneurial spirit. We became an extension of their own dreams. They were captivated by our total conviction in our cause, our confidence that we could achieve sometimes daunting goals, and our full commitment to do whatever was necessary to succeed. They sensed the "primal force" that propels an entrepreneur. We gave them the opportunity to relive the entrepreneurial experience vicariously through us. When people puzzle over how we were able to "get in the door" of some large corporations and get a seat at the senior executive table, I respond that there was no magic involved. Executives like to associate with individuals who have high energy, initiative, and willingness to take the risk of striking out on their own. They like to be associated with the potential for success. Who doesn't?

A secondary but important benefit of having a relationship with a senior executive is as a safeguard against bureaucratic quicksand. Large organizations have departments that exist only to protect against all eventualities, especially legal ones. Often they are populated with staff members who have reached a plateau in their climb up the corporate ladder. These middle managers have become "lifers" who spend more time finding problems than providing creative solutions. Curiously, they are often involved in negotiations and later become the bureaucratic gatekeepers of agreements. They can be the bane of an entrepreneur's existence. For me, the most effective way to survive a conflict with such middle managers was by maintaining my direct access to the top leader. That executive and I could see beyond the minutiae and focus our attention on what was really relevant to success.

When you are about to take the plunge, ask yourself: do you find an irresistible joy in talking about your dream? Are you able to captivate your audience with your energy and enthusiasm? Do you reach out to others and bring them into your "fold" as you invite them to participate in the adventure? Do you love to dance and feel at ease with the give-and-take of it? If you answered yes to all of these, I'd say you are ready.

Regards,

Ricardo

3

Absorbing Uncertainty:
The Entrepreneurial Covenant

Perhaps the entrepreneur's most crucial leadership role is to absorb uncertainty, thus allowing others to fully participate in the journey. In doing so, the leader and the participant enter into a covenant, part of the fabric of the enterprise. This fabric sustains and nourishes the organization in times of difficulty and energizes it in times of success.

When you become comfortable with uncertainty, infinite possibilities open up in your life. It means fear is no longer a dominant factor in what you do and no longer prevents you from taking action to initiate change. The Roman philosopher Tacitus rightly observed that "the desire for safety stands against every great and noble enterprise." If uncertainty is unacceptable to you, it turns into fear. If it is perfectly acceptable, it turns into increased aliveness, alertness, and creativity.

ECKHART TOLLE

Dear Entrepreneur:

*I*F YOU ASKED WHETHER RISK entered my decision to leave a reasonably secure and predictable position with a large corporation and step into a new venture, my immediate response would be that my decision was not at all about risk. It was about conviction. Yet this question would be appropriate, because risk is involved in any new venture, and an important measure of an entrepreneur's leadership capability is the manner in which he or she absorbs risk on behalf of the organization.

Each of us has a different appetite for risk. The entrepreneur may have a higher-than-average appetite. At first, I felt the excitement of the high stakes involved in starting a business and the rush of engaging in a totally new endeavor. Risk assessment did not even enter my mind. Once I reached the *entrepreneurial tipping point*, a sense of certainty that we would succeed removed my concern about risk. The fact that wealth was never one of my criteria for success helped. My goals transcended simple financial gain; they were much broader and thus more meaningful to me.

At the same time, it was very important not to overlook—and thus minimize—the sense of risk that others may have felt when asked to join our enterprise. We were driving, so we could anticipate the curves and detours, or at least we had control over when to turn. But that was not the case with all the passengers, especially new ones. Some who joined had a large tolerance for risk and therefore were fully capable of sharing the driving. Others put their full trust in us as they boarded the vehicle. That trust let them reconcile their risk tolerance with the unknowns of the journey and permitted them to be effective—and contributing—participants while our vehicle took on the vagaries of the road.

Trust in the leadership is a very important aspect of any enterprise. A key part of being a leader is to help those who join the business *feel at ease with uncertainty*. In a very real sense they are entrusting us, the entrepreneurs, with their destiny, and we provide a certain level of security that they are making the right decision. It is not unlike the trust we place in a bank when we deposit funds. Individuals who join us are making a deposit as part of their commitment to participate in the adventure, a deposit of *trust packets*.

The size of the deposit depends on the individual's self-confidence and role in the enterprise. Some join without hesitation, fully engaged in the vision and confident that they will contribute to making that vision a reality. Others, while intrigued, are by nature more cautious and hesitant. They need more reassurance, and they place greater reliance on the leader to be "right." The size of their trust deposits is, therefore, larger, and the leader carries a greater support burden for those individuals. The good leader senses this difference in capacity for uncertainty and adjusts the exchange accordingly. The capacity for uncertainty also becomes a criterion for determining the best roles for individual participants, considering not only their specific professional skills but also their ability to assist with the driving.

Confidence in the face of uncertainty goes well beyond co-workers. How often have you faced an investor and answered the question "Can it be done?" with an unwavering "I believe it can." That is the moment when you took a little (or big) trust packet from that investor. When you take this deposit seriously, and you give depositors the peace of mind to go home believing that you will do everything in your capacity to honor their trust, you are discharging one of your most important leadership jobs. You are truly carrying the leadership mantle.

However, with this mantle comes a very large and often poorly understood obligation: every "trust deposit" someone makes with you creates a link, like a thread in a fabric being woven, and each link establishes a special relationship that I consider a "covenant" with that person. Much like the biblical covenant, this one is an understanding of faith and trust, monitored purely within yourself, defining your responsibility and behavior relative to that person. In fact, as you grow a company, you create a fabric of covenants. That fabric becomes an intangible power that unites and strengthens an organization when times are tough and lubricates it when times are good.[5]

One of the most significant "fabric-building" commitments I made occurred when our company sought its first external financing. We had established a reputation as a high-caliber research organization, able to contribute new ideas to some of the most prestigious corporate research labs in our field. Our clients included Monsanto, Dow, Shell Oil, Mobil Oil, even Exxon, the very company that Jim and I had come from. We were now ready to develop our own technology, and we needed major financial backing. One of our key board members introduced us to Tommy Davis, a dean of the venture capital community who had pioneered the field in the 1970s.[6] Although his venture group's expertise was not in our business, he was willing to talk to us on the strength of our board member's introduction. I presented our case, backed by data, references, and solid financial projections. But in the end it was the personal connection created between us that led to his belief in us as entrepreneurs. He made a bet on us as individuals. When he did, I felt that I had entered into a covenant with him. I saw the import of his acceptance and the significance of his trust, and I felt responsible for meeting his expectations.

A decade later that trust was rewarded with financial return for him and his venture group. But the relationship was much more than just a financial transaction. It was a bond between executives, which became part of the fabric of our company as well as his. The covenant was mutual, and its reciprocity would be demonstrated many times in subsequent years. One example was that Tommy overrode the then-typical requirement that venture investments become salable within three to four years. From the outset, we made it clear that support for our venture would require a commitment of at least a decade. Another time, when Olin Corporation backed out of supporting us at the very last minute, after a long negotiation, Tommy was the venture investor who declared, "The next deal will be even better!"

I describe my financing experiences only to illustrate that they were so clearly based on *trust*. While investors certainly computed the financial potential of the company in making their decisions, they ultimately bet on individuals. As my friend and colleague Martin McGlynn, CEO of Stem Cells, Inc., points out: "VCs who invest in new technology plays have relatively little to go by, except the founders and management team. They typically bet on the jockey, not the horse. They trust the jockey."

As we guide our companies through difficult development stages, we create a "wake" that sweeps essential constituents along the path: co-workers, investors, suppliers, customers, and the local communities in which we work. In the process, we weave an intricate fabric. Its fibers are an invisible web of interdependencies that, while associated with the company, are embodied in all employees but most intensely in the persona of the leader.

The leader is at the apex of a pyramid of trust, the standard bearer. This important, intangible responsibility, awesome in its significance, is often unrecognized and certainly not sufficiently praised, yet it is part of the beauty and meaning of entrepreneurial leadership.[7]

Regards,

Ricardo

4

Contrasting Forces— Optimism versus Realism

An entrepreneur faces powerful contrasting forces that influence most actions: exuberant optimism and hard realism, action orientation and quiet reflection, the clamor for expedient decisions and the need for cautious rigor in evaluating options. The challenge is how to live with these forces while maintaining internal sanity and external integrity. You cannot always meet that challenge by yourself.

When you encounter difficulties and contradictions, do not try
to break them, but bend them with gentleness and time.

SAINT FRANCIS DE SALES

Dear Entrepreneur:

$\mathcal{T}$RUST PACKETS ARE NOT THE ONLY "weight" on an entrepreneurial leader's shoulders. Innumerable opposing forces confront us as we move our dream forward and face some of the hard realities of the business world. Coping with these forces becomes its own dance, choreographed between opposing requirements that sometimes seem impossible to reconcile.

For me, perhaps one of the most difficult issues has been between exuberant optimism—a fundamental energizing aspect of the entrepreneur—and harsh realism—a requirement for facing real-life limitations. I confronted my most vivid tension of opposites when I was developing key corporate relationships with other companies while being hampered by severe fiscal limitations at my own company. It is hard enough to convince a large corporate partner to do business with a small company, but it is even harder when your financial "runway" is counted in months rather than years. Moving negotiations forward with such a potential partner requires an upbeat, optimistic demeanor and an unwavering can-do attitude. Facing fiscal uncertainty at the office takes great composure and the ability to soberly assess options and priorities without losing hope.

The issue of balancing opposites arises not only in the financial realm. As your team assesses technical hurdles in the development cycle of a new product, inevitably major unknowns need to be resolved. When the path to solution seems nowhere in sight, you rely on hope and confidence that your superb technical team will find the answers in time. You can't afford to let the difficulties sap your energy, especially if you are simultaneously promoting your company as you seek capital and woo partners. So, while you show a positive external face glowing with confidence, you need to "park" within yourself your technical staff's messages of concern about the difficulty ahead. Another trust packet to put in your leadership backpack.

For me, being positive has always come naturally. Even in the most difficult situations, my inner default response is to find the silver lining. While this has served me well as I built companies and advised younger leaders, it also has a serious shortcoming: it can become a soothing balm that lets me cope with and sometimes obscure—or even hide—harsh realities. When this happens, I can become insensitive to others who are immersed in the difficulties. This insensitivity can be a serious problem if optimism becomes a crutch used to avoid facing hard truths.

I remember a number of instances during the development of our Xonon combustion technology when Ralph Dalla Betta, the inventor and senior scientist on the project, came to me with news of a major failure in our system. My response was, "I know you will figure it out." I had enormous faith in Ralph, whom I had worked with for many years, ever since we were graduate students together at Stanford. My reply worked for me at that moment, as it saved me from falling into a well of worry—after all, so much was riding on continuing progress in that project. But it did not sit well with Ralph. Fortunately, I had a deep enough understanding of the science to believe that the project could be done, even if neither he nor I had any idea how, at that moment. However, my attitude certainly did not leave any room for failure, and that made it difficult for Ralph and others to feel fully "heard."

It is natural for us to listen to what we want to hear, a form of ego self-protection. And people around us may likewise want to avoid conveying unpleasant facts. Sometimes they downplay bad news for their own self-interest, sometimes because they want to protect us. The result is the same: we, who should be privy to all the facts, are given only part of the story, and it takes significant inner fortitude to press for the whole truth—unpleasant as it may be.

Both inclinations—optimism and realism—are needed. Most of us are much better at one than the other. It is therefore wise to surround ourselves with people who complement our skills. For me it was colleagues with greater capacity to confront hard realities.[8] I was fortunate in this regard, but I also worked at understanding—and overcoming—the blind spot that my optimistic nature creates: succumbing to my need for control and for immediate action plans when faced with a dilemma. When I confront a major issue, a lack of alternative solutions stresses me and drains my energy. Rather than accepting the reality that, at that moment, I do not see an immediate resolution—and letting it be—I immediately begin to imagine alternatives that could resolve the situation. This gives me a feeling of forward movement and satisfies my need for a sense of control. My behavior has an upside and a downside: action orientation is a valuable trait; haste is not. The optimism–realism set of contrasting forces is shadowed by the action–reflection set. The optimist is more likely to rush into action; the realist may be paralyzed by analysis. Neither is optimal.

For me, turning to wise and candid colleagues was one path for resolving this internal tension. Another path, even better because it is always available, is to create moments in my day when I overtly release control and diminish my thirst for action in my optimistic exuberance. Sometimes I achieve this by exercise. But most often meditation has been my companion. Regular practice of quieting my mind and subduing my inner restlessness has allowed me to experience moments when my need for action is totally suspended.[9] The insights that followed have convinced me of the value of awareness of my unrelenting need to be in control. Meditation has also confirmed something that one of my business mentors, Dick Fleming, taught me: while we may think we need to act, many times that expectation is purely a creation of our own minds. Postponing action not only is quite often possible but also enables new insights and new solutions to surface. My friend Martin McGlynn reminds me of this by quoting John Milton: "They also serve who only stand and wait" and the so appropriate Eagles' song "Learn to Be Still."

> It's just another day in paradise
> As you stumble to your bed
> You'd give anything to silence
> Those voices ringing in your head
> You thought you could find happiness
> Just over that green hill
> You thought you would be satisfied
> But you never will—
> Learn to be still.

On the optimism–realism spectrum, where does each entrepreneur fit? For some the answer is clear. Take my partner Jim Cusumano. With no hesitation I place him far on the optimism side. For me, the answer is not as clear anymore. While my inclination has been to join the optimistic camp, I find that it depends on where those around me stand on the spectrum. For example, when I am with Jim, I naturally become the realistic counterbalance to his exuberance. However, when I am with people who lack the optimistic component and are more focused on the hard realities, I move into optimistic mode. This is not calculated. It happens naturally, as I sense the situation and strive for balance. As I grow older and my role changes from acting to guiding, I find this flexibility welcome. I encourage you to study your behavior in this regard, primarily to be aware of the dimensions you are missing and to find them. You can achieve balance between optimism and realism by being aware of your biases and by having members of your team who complement your style and predisposition.

Regards,

Ricardo

5

The Pull of Hubris

The tension between hubris and humility is one of the most serious personal dilemmas faced by the entrepreneur. Hubris, the point at which self-confidence turns into conceit, can be a trap in which we lose our bearings, with destructive consequences not just for ourselves but also for many others. To keep in balance we need to maintain a spiritual anchor and manifest that core in our moral and ethical behavior.

Humility is the foundation of all the other virtues. Hence, in the soul in which this virtue does not exist, there cannot be any other virtue except in mere appearance.

SAINT AUGUSTINE

Dear Entrepreneur:

WHILE TEAM MEMBERS MAY assist with the balance between optimism and realism, such external help is not available for one of the most serious struggles a leader faces: the tension between hubris and humility. Maintaining humility in the face of growth and success requires very hard inner work. The contrasting force, hubris, needs to be constantly tamed. Continuous reflection is required to resist the tendency of power to corrupt our humility and our humanity. It is a battle that tests the best in us.

This issue became very prominent to many people several years ago, when our world was shaken by a number of corporate disasters: Tyco, WorldCom, and Enron. In one instance, the effects of hubris touched me directly. In 1995, Enron invested in the energy subsidiary I had co-founded, and it became an important strategic corporate partner. That relationship ended in 2000—fortunately before Enron's collapse but certainly not before we had become closely acquainted with several of its senior managers and affected by their company's behavior.

When the Enron story was unraveling, I continued to believe strongly that the senior executives whom I knew were not aware of the improper financial manipulations in their company or they would not have remained a part of it.

While in cases like this ignorance is not an excuse, since it flies in the face of executive responsibility, I did not believe that these individuals were acting with malicious intent or for personal gain to the detriment of their employees, shareholders, and customers. I still believe this, although many of my colleagues argue that I was somewhat blinded by my pervasive optimism and belief in the best from everyone. Indeed, as the magnitude of the Enron case and the other corporate disasters became more evident, it was increasingly difficult to have faith in executive integrity. In spite of this, I still contend that much of what happened was the result of missteps, fear, the seductive force of growing power, and hubris. My conclusion does not excuse the behavior, but it explains it.

Hubris has many faces. In the extreme, the Greeks defined it as actions that defy the gods. More generally, it refers to acts of pride, superciliousness, or arrogance resulting from misplaced and excessive self-confidence. For me, it is the point when *self-confidence* turns to *conceit*, defined by the *Oxford English Dictionary* as an overweening opinion of oneself, overestimation of one's own qualities, personal vanity, or pride. Hubris, if just contained within an individual, can be irrelevant (or at least harmless), but when it affects others it becomes a very dangerous force.

I have said previously that self-confidence is an essential quality of an entrepreneur. When it evolves into conceit—when hubris takes over—it is a trap with destructive consequences for us and many others involved in our business efforts. This is why I see hubris as perhaps the most difficult and serious of the contrasting forces a leader encounters— and one that only the leader can resolve. While people surrounding us may sound alerts and wake-up calls if we trespass into the hubris zone, in the end the pull of hubris needs to be confronted personally. At a certain point the confrontation acquires great urgency, since, as leaders, we cast long shadows in our companies, and our hubris can permeate the culture of the whole organization. That is what I surmise happened at Enron.

I liken hubris to a virus that starts at the top and spreads throughout a company. Just as the effective leader can and must inject the organization with passion and enthusiasm, he or she can also shift the whole organization's energy into negative territory. And the shift can be hard to see until it has become pervasive. When we get a little too enamored with success, it is as if we start breathing different oxygen, a con- taminated oxygen with a molecular makeup that is some- what distorted. As this distorted oxygen spreads around the company and all the employees continue to breathe the com- pany air, they are not aware that they are also slowly ingest- ing this defective gas, one that is more and more removed from the real world. The toxicity may reach a level where there is no antidote. Under those conditions, we may start to believe that the rules do not apply to us, that our seeming success is proof that we are not only right but also above the law. We are in danger of losing our moral, ethical, and, for that matter, *spiritual* anchor. The change is often imperceptible to us and to others until it is too late.

What goes wrong? The leader fails to be watchful over the inner battle between hubris and humility. A good leader is aware of this inner danger and makes sure that signposts, internal and external, are present to permit timely correction. A good partner who acts as a signpost is a godsend. But the most important signpost is self-awareness.

I had an early warning. The company I had founded was young, imbued with enthusiasm and a level of naiveté. We threw a holiday party for all our employees and spouses. At one point I was dancing with one of our employees, and I overheard her husband say that I was dancing as if I owned the world. Most likely he meant it as a compliment, but I sensed an edge. I was taking over the floor, displaying a self-confidence and self-assurance that was insensitive to the "space" of others. I was touching the edge of conceit. I was at that imperceptible border where, instead of being sensitive to the needs and feelings of others—my more natural persona—I was caught up in my own world. I was feeling too good, too full of myself. This was a warning sign that I have never forgotten. What impressed me most was how a seemingly insignificant remark could be such a significant call. Warnings like this come from what poet Rodger Kamenetz refers to as the Elijahs we meet in daily life.[10]

As I think back to the Enron experience, even in the

early years of our interactions with the executives there—
and many years before Enron's collapse—a sense prevailed
within their organization that nothing could stop them, that
they had the key to the future. Was it self-confidence or was
it conceit? It is hard to tell. What I believe in retrospect is
that I should have been more aware of the difference and
more mindful of its consequences. While I probably would
not have changed the overall nature of the relationship, I
would have built in additional safeguards to preserve my
own organization's well-being in case the ugly head of hubris
prevailed.

I would also have been more alert. One of Enron's projects
was going to be the main demonstration site for installation
of our Xonon system in large General Electric turbines,[11]
a key factor in GE's interest in our innovation. Even well
before Enron's downfall, the project seemed to falter with no
clear technical or business cause, and we never knew clearly
what was leading to the shift in priorities. In retrospect, I
suspect the shift may well have been part of Enron's constant
financial games. Had we been more alert to the dynamics
within Enron, perhaps we would have looked more actively
for alternative partners.

The times I *was* more watchful actually saved our company. In one case in 1982, it was in fact the chief negotiator on
the other side who insisted that a clause be put into our final
agreement protecting us if the deal was derailed at the last
minute. He displayed his full belief in our dream and was a

true "dance partner." As it turned out, the CEO of his large company did renege at the very last moment. We survived because of the significant financial penalty and the insight of that good and wise friend. His name was Roy Kesting, and I salute him for his wisdom to this day. I was fortunate that I had advisers and colleagues like Roy, who balanced my optimistic bias when I most needed it.

In another instance, several years later, our CEO at the time, Dick Fleming, and our attorney, Larry Sonsini, made sure that we added a protective contract clause in our growing relationship with Koch Industries. While I was very enthusiastic about the potential of the partnership (and had a hard time conceiving of failure), both Dick and Larry felt that, as a small company, we needed protection in case of a sudden change of heart by our powerful partner—whether because of hubris or because of a plain shift in strategy. Koch did suddenly back out many years later, and, had it not been for this provision, we probably would have gone under.

Regards,

Ricardo

6

Spiritual Awareness and the
Treasure of Meditation

A spiritual anchor is fundamental to our leadership skill—whether we are conscious of it or not. It is the link that transcends the external forces of the moment. It permits us to cope with success without losing our humility and to face failure without losing our self-esteem. The practice of meditation permits us to quiet our minds and get in touch with our ethical and moral compass. This makes us better leaders.

Better indeed is knowledge than mechanical practice. Better than knowledge is meditation. But better still is surrender of attachment to results, because there follows immediate peace.

THE BHAGAVAD GITA

Dear Entrepreneur:

*Y*OU MAY ASK WHEN I MOST experienced the pull of hubris and what helped me "get through it." Without a doubt, the greatest challenge raised its head when my company grew tenfold. We had already been in business for over two decades, slowly progressing from a "boutique" research organization to a company serving the pharmaceutical industry with research, development, and small-scale manufacturing. Then we undertook a two-year path of acquisitions, including a substantial facility that made us one of the largest outsourcing suppliers in the industry. Almost overnight I found myself the CEO of a public company with 1,800 employees and locations all around the United States. This was hardly what I had been trained for, and I often wondered how "this little Jewish boy from South America" had come so far. I was trained as an engineer, someone who thrived uncovering novel applications for new and interesting compounds, a scientist who would spend hours doing experiments and pondering the meaning of results. Yet here I was at the head of a company with hundreds of millions of dollars in sales, being picked up by limos and hobnobbing with executives who owned private jets—with lots of opportunity to contaminate my oxygen.

So, how did I keep my oxygen clean? Perhaps the most

important factor was being surrounded in both my family and my business by people who did not forget their roots. Yes, we were all proud of what we had achieved, but we were equally cognizant that we were just one part of a very large, very complex industry. And we did not forget that we had started from nothing and traveled a long and difficult road to get to where we now were. My immediate family still lived in Ecuador, and my childhood friends, whom I saw regularly, were still part of a small community of immigrants who had left Europe during World War II under difficult circumstances.

It also helped that around this time one of my friends, Professor André Delbecq at the Santa Clara University Business School, was developing a pioneering program that he titled Spirituality in Business Leadership. He sought to address, from the vantage point of personal beliefs, the challenges of business in modern societies: decision-making and discernment problems; the importance of reflection, contemplation, and meditation; and the challenges of power, wealth, and greed.[12] The concept intrigued me, because I had long believed that effectiveness as a leader was intimately related to inner spiritual, moral, and ethical anchors. As André shared with me the framework for his course, I had a chance to see something articulated that until then had been just in the back of my mind. Subsequently, he asked me to be part of the first session of the course, which allowed me to formally examine practices that would help improve my personal behavior and leadership skills.[13]

Not surprisingly, the hubris–humility dynamic was a very important theme in André's curriculum and involved hands-on experiences appropriate to the very personal nature of the subject. Perhaps the most dramatic of these for me was that each business student was asked to personally touch the less fortunate in our society as a reminder of the difficulties and challenges faced by others—a form of "grounding" from the sometimes lofty thin air of business. My choice was clear: the homeless. For a long time I had been troubled by my tendency to avoid the people in sleeping bags on city streets, making big detours around them. I remembered vividly the times when, while walking back to my luxury hotel from business dinners in New York City, I would avoid eye contact with the poor people who were settling down on Fifth Avenue for the night. I was shunning fellow human beings. What was I really afraid of?

André's invitation gave me a chance to confront this head-on. I decided to spend time at a homeless shelter, helping to serve food and getting to know the residents. After the meal, I would sit and talk with different individuals. The experience touched me deeply and has stayed with me ever since. Some of the residents did not have a good handle on what I consider "reality" and probably needed to be taken care of at mental institutions. Others were purely out of luck, having lost their jobs and being unable to pay for a room. Although the shelter strictly forbade drug use, it was also clear that many had serious addiction problems. But they all were human beings like me, and their humanity was evident when we sat eye to eye and shoulder to shoulder. The experience was humbling and sharpened in me the sense of compassion that is so important a part of being human.

Another very important theme of the course was the pressing need for leaders to set aside quiet time. How often have I wished to take a walk in the woods or go to the beach and watch the waves, yet I did not do it, using the excuse that I did not have time. Even when I tried to get away, I found it almost impossible to shut my mind to the demands of the office, because of either the ever-expanding reach of communication technology or simply the perpetual chatter of my mind. Since reflective opportunities are scarce in our culture, André's course emphasized the importance of creating structured time to quiet the mind, achieving some measure of inner silence as an essential tonic for better performance of our leadership responsibilities.

André put forth a very simple challenge: commit to practice meditation twenty minutes every day for twenty days: 20/20. If this practice did not show clear results, we were free to drop it. For me, the practice took hold and was remarkably uncomplicated. Over time, I would become acquainted with various forms of meditation, but in the end what mattered most was giving my mind permission to stop talking to me and taking a real break, a time-out. Meditation became a way to re-focus on the moment, which often involved taming my enthusiasm and excitement and letting go of my expectations. It allowed me to be quietly present, with no intrusion from things I should have done in the past or tasks I had to do in the future.

As pointed out by several spiritual teachers, stopping the chatter of the mind has another positive consequence: it interrupts the mind's tendency to create scenarios with limited information, often prematurely transforming bits of input into whole "truths" that then influence our attitudes and our behavior. This process is expressed well by Buddhist writer Pema Chodron, who asks: "How do we catch our thoughts before they become 100% believable?"[14] and by Rabbi Alan Lew, who explores the views of Jewish commentators:

We imagine that something presents a threat to us, or that we can't control it, or that it might impinge on our being. This thought may very well have a more visceral root, but by the time it reaches our awareness, it is a formal construct, a melodrama made of language. We lose sight of the breath. We develop an excessive—and absolute—belief in the reality of a particular form—an idea, a construct—and this belief blocks the possibility of fluidity, the ongoingness of the breath. That is why when we fall into a panic, people instinctively tell us, "Just take a deep breath." Breathing is more primal, more real than form. Breath calms us down, relieves pain, and expands our awareness, creating space for us, relieving us from the contracted and limited world of language and concept.[15]

For me meditation, like the breath, permits me to gain perspective, to recognize when all I am doing with my thoughts is creating "melodramas made of language."

Often, when I bring up the subject of meditation, I sense interest but also a feeling of mystery and even reservation. The assumption (and fear that accompanies it) is that meditation is an esoteric Eastern practice of some intangible sort, associated with cultish elements, and not applicable to our rational thinking in Western society. For me there is really nothing magical or mysterious or weird about this practice. I envision it as a delightful inner stroll, a leisurely walk that I like to take alone. When the plethora of thoughts that crowd my everyday mind want to accompany me, I set them aside gently, to be picked up later. To manage distractions, I use a word—a sort of mantra—as many meditation practices suggest.[16] Repeating this word helps me re-focus when my mind wanders. It also helps me interrupt the chatter I hear in my busy mind—the problem solving, the worry—so that my mind lets me be, for these brief minutes. That is all there is to it.[17]

Most meditation practitioners stress the importance of a posture that permits free breathing and good body balance; for me what works best is to sit upright comfortably on a pillow, cross-legged. I find it very important not to get upset when I catch my mind being nasty and insisting on intruding. I notice it and then go back to the meditation, accepting this as part of my learning. The important thing is to stay the course. Afterward I often feel refreshed and renewed, even exuberant. But sometimes I do not notice any difference—and I accept that. I do know that my wife can tell when I have not meditated. Something in my demeanor and tone betrays it, maybe an edginess that creeps in during times of tension. I feel fortunate that she encourages my practice. By now my children and grandchildren have caught on to what I'm doing, and when they see me sitting in a corner with my eyes closed they respect the solitude. (Even my dog has become used to this routine and simply sits next to me—facing the same direction, as if something were there that is important to watch.)

Meditating every day has become habitual for me. It provides me with a wonderful daily "energizer" and creates a refuge during overload. Sometimes, when hard issues press on me or I am unable to see solutions to dilemmas, I quiet my mind by going into meditation. Greater clarity often follows.[18]

This practice was very important to me when we received an offer to buy our company several years after our dramatic growth. The offer confronted me with many conflicting considerations. On the upside, if consummated, the transaction would enable me to meet my fiduciary responsibility. In addition to assuring a good return for our shareholders, it ensured that the company could continue to grow in an increasingly demanding and capital-intensive industry. On the downside, life for our employees—and for me—would change dramatically. Many had come to work for us because they were seeking an exciting entrepreneurial group that would give them a real say in the destiny of the company, something larger corporate organizations lacked. This was the very same desire to be in charge that had motivated me to create the company in the first place twenty-five years earlier. Now I was about to turn the clock back.

What most concerned me was whether this sale was fully consistent with my covenant with the people who had entrusted me with leadership of the company, the people whose "trust packets" I carried. Also, of course, I had to come to terms with my personal issue, the "other side of the coin" of the entrepreneurial growth spirit: was I ready to quit?

Meditation was instrumental in my conclusion of this complex transaction; it was an ally in the decision-making process. After weighing all the options, I decided to pursue the deal. My conviction that this was the right path for us enabled me to convince the skeptics on our board of directors, even though many still felt the tug to stay independent and to grow further. We completed the negotiations during the last days of December 2000, ten months after the first contact about the buyout. As it turned out, the following year unfolded as a very difficult one for our industry and the world. We had made the right decision at the right time. In particular, I am at peace that the decision was the best for our employees, as it placed the company with a group that had the financial capacity to overcome the difficulties and come out stronger and more focused.

Another palpable benefit of my meditation practice during this tough period was my increased ability to be more open, sensitive, and fully available to those around me, despite the tension and complexity of the moment. It allowed me to convey a level of calm to the company, sometimes simply by smiling when I walked in the door or by offering a good word to a colleague who was struggling with an issue—personal or professional. My executive assistant Linda McGee—who was better tuned in to the mood of the employees than I was—would sometimes poke her head into my office and suggest that I talk to Charlie or Jean because they seemed "down." Just giving brief attention to troubled colleagues lightened their burden, reminding them that I, as CEO, carried some of their trust packets and that I continued to be the everyday "glue" of the organization.

Regular meditation also influenced my demeanor in these negotiations. At a critical point, when strong disagreements between the financial officers of the two companies threatened to derail the deal, my intervention with a compassionate and empathetic rather than antagonistic spirit saved the day. We had been negotiating for many months. The head of the European company, Jan Zuidam, had agreed to the basic terms. Yet our negotiating teams were trapped in details, unable to reach closure. This seemed in part due to objections from the senior financial officer of the buyout company, who, in the eyes of our own CFO, was always negative and obstructive and did not want to do the deal in the first place. (Maybe the other side felt the same about our CFO.)

It reached a point where I felt the agreement was going to fall apart. I was very upset, especially since we had put an enormous amount of time and energy into it, at considerable financial and emotional expense for a relatively small company. I decided to call Jan, but first I spent time in quiet, trying to place myself in the other company's mind-set.

When I finally made the call, I was not confrontational. On the contrary, I projected as best I could what must be going on in his organization, feeling enormous empathy for the decision-making challenges that Jan was facing "at home." It was one of the best conversations we ever had (even though it happened by phone across nine time zones), and the next day my CFO told me that the negotiations were back on track. I am convinced that my reflective, empathetic, and optimistic attitude played a very important role in this outcome. I was able to discern the forces acting on both sides and act appropriately.

If you are not yet a practitioner of meditation, I encourage you to try the 20/20 rule. I expect that it will pay good dividends, as it did for me. And remember, whether you call it meditation or not, finding quiet time is essential for leadership sanity and effectiveness.

Regards,

Ricardo

7

Discernment and the Predicament of Control

The need for control is one of the most pervasive personal issues for many business leaders. While control gives direction to the organization, it can impair our ability to be open to new avenues and opportunities or even to be fully aware of threats and dangers. It can seriously limit our discernment capability and reduce our leadership effectiveness.

The law of detachment ... says that in order to acquire any-thing in the physical universe, you have to relinquish your attachment to it. This doesn't mean you give up the intention to create your desire. You give up your attachment to the result.

DEEPAK CHOPRA

◇

We must love them both, those whose opinions we share and those whose opinions we reject. For both have labored in the search for truth and both have helped us in the finding of it.

SAINT THOMAS AQUINAS

Dear Entrepreneur:

THE WORD DISCERNMENT CAPTURES A subtle but very important quality of the accomplished leader. I consider it an extension of "gut feel," the term often used when we cannot articulate the rationale for our actions. In contrast to *judgment*, which to me connotes an intellectual process that carefully weighs the pros and cons of a situation, discernment is much more an intuitive feeling, something driven by a deep source within us. Yet it is no less deliberate, even if we are at times at a loss to explain why we are suddenly driven to act in a particular way.

While actions based on discernment may seem sudden, if they are about subjects important to us they actually arise from a continuous "behind the scenes" activity within us. Quiet and mostly unconscious, they coalesce from a constant flow of thoughts and feelings that relate to the issue we are confronting or considering. The action points are just the nexus of this inner activity. They remind me of Iguazu Falls. Several rivers from the surrounding mountains in Brazil, Paraguay, and Argentina come together in a broad, placid, smoothly flowing Iguazu river delta that is perhaps two miles wide. The water is so calm that when I was there I boarded a canoe and slowly drifted toward the barely visible islands downstream. Little did I appreciate, as I neared the islands, the drama that would soon unfold. Suddenly, a few feet beyond the islands, the water cascaded into an extraordinary and magnificent semicircular gorge to produce one of the great marvels of the natural world. The water was inexorably flowing through the delta with no significant indication of the massive, concentrated, spectacular feature that was about to appear. It is the same with the discernment process, which is mostly hidden. When I confront a serious topic that I care about, my mind will become active even if I am not consciously considering the subject. The thoughts are bathing me all the time, permeating my conscious and subconscious mind like the waters in a broad delta. Then, when the moment is right, I am driven to act.

Not long ago I was at a board meeting where one of the members was going to formalize his retirement. We had talked about it off and on over the previous months, and as we gathered for the meeting the general sense was that this would be our colleague's last meeting. The executive, a prominent leader in the energy industry, had served on the board for many years and was shifting his efforts to non-profit work. While I understood and went along with his decision, deep inside me something was nagging. I did not know what it was until the instant the discussion turned to his retirement at that meeting. In that moment I "knew" that this was not the best time for his resignation; it was coming at a delicate point in the company's growth. Almost in spite of myself I suggested that he might want to delay his retirement. As it turned out, my unplanned intervention was perfectly timed, because it read the circumstances accurately and articulated what was in many people's minds. There was no need for discussion. The executive accepted. It felt like an "of course!" moment. The river had reached the critical point.

Discernment skill differentiates a great leader from a good leader: discernment—and a sixth sense for the timing of an action. Am I good at it? Not always. My biggest obstacle is a need to be in control. It often gets in the way of letting my subconscious do its discernment work. The need to control comes from two related factors: a restless impatience to see my plans realized, and a discomfort when there is no clear path forward.

Like many entrepreneurs, I hold a strong conviction that I know best what needs to be done, and I often would rather do it myself than trust the task to others. I am the captain, and I need to have my hands on the wheel. I "know" the right destination and the best path, and I want everyone to follow it, exactly. Displaying confidence that I am steering the ship is important, but the danger comes when I am so convinced that the ship's immediate direction is right that I get lulled into thinking that I really am the complete master of the ship's destiny. By exerting too much control, I may be severely limiting the outcome. In fact, by intervening too soon I may not see many of the possibilities or dangers.

That intervention narrows the range of possible outcomes is a well-known phenomenon in physics. In the late

1920s, when quantum physics was in its infancy, a key concept in understanding the experimental observations was the uncertainty principle. Werner Heisenberg, a brilliant young physicist, postulated that it was not possible to know both the position and the velocity of the electron at the same time. This contradicted the belief of many luminaries, such as Niels Bohr, who had first proposed the structure of the atom. Heisenberg's principle eventually proved correct and applied to a much broader context than just physics. In his words, "In the sharp formulation of the causality law—if we know the present, then we can predict the future—it is not the *consequence*, but the *premise* that is false. As a matter of principle, we cannot know all determining elements of the present."[19]

I may feel in command of the direction in which I am navigating. Yet I have limited knowledge of all the factors at play and can only *hope* that the future happens as I envision it. When I am too fixed on an outcome and push too hard, I may in fact be changing the very result that I hope for—just as the act of measuring the position of the electron affects its velocity. Fixation on an outcome can also lead to blindness to alternative paths, severely limiting the decision process.

I recognize now that some of my need for control is related to a lack of comfort with being in the unknown. This is surprising, since as a scientist I am continuously fascinated with problems that have no obvious solution. It would seem to follow that I thrive in unknown territory. This may have been true in my scientific work in the past, but it is not so true in my business life. I now believe that instances of my deep unease with uncertainty may have hampered some of my business creativity. I am clearly not alone in this. Julian Gresser, who advised our young executive team in the 1970s, wrote in *Piloting through Chaos*:

This ability to be at ease in the unknown is also one of the links to true creativity. This recalls Keats's statement about living with uncertainty: "It struck me what quality went to form the Man of Achievement, especially in Literature, and which Shakespeare possessed so enormously—I mean Negative Capability, that is, when a man is capable of being in uncertainties, mysteries, and doubts, without any irritable reaching after fact and reason." This no irritable reaching after fact and reason holds a clue not only to creative expression in the arts; it is also the mark of the martial arts and the skills of great negotiators. For when you are loose and light, your heart open and your body peaceful and happy, the openings—especially in the darkness—come to you, and in legions when you least expect them, and then resistance gives way.[20]

My impatience is often very "irritable" and hampers my ability to discern well. This relates to an aspect of my need for control that I have often puzzled over: the difference between *self-confidence* and *self-esteem*. When I am telling the story of my ideas and dreams, I exude certainty and conviction: I exude *self-confidence*. Such self-confidence is essential for entrepreneurial success. But it alone is not enough. Success would be very limited if I were not open to the ideas of others, open to facts I may have overlooked, and open to paths that might be different from mine. Receptivity to such differences requires a certain inner resilience, a willingness to recognize shortcomings, and a willingness to change direction. It requires humility to receive different views fully, even when they question the views that I so self-confidently express. To do so requires a strong measure of *self-esteem*: a level of comfort with who I am—with my gifts and my warts—a level of self-love that translates into a greater ease in letting go of control and being comfortable with not-knowing.[21]

Meditation has helped me increase my comfort with the state of not-knowing and be more receptive to the inner signals of discernment. The trick for me has been to extend this ability beyond the quiet of my meditation sanctuary and into active life. The need for this is beautifully expressed in a poem by sixteenth-century Buddhist Hung Ying-ming, author of the *Ts'ai-ken T'an* (literally, "vegetable root discourses," meaning thoughts about a simple life):

> *The stillness*
> *in stillness*
> *is not stillness.*
> *Only when*

there is stillness
in movement
can the spiritual rhythm appear
which pervades
heaven and earth.[22]

Twentieth-century rabbi Abraham Joshua Heschel also talks about quiet in action when he relates awe to "the stillness of the eternal" amid "the rush of the passing":

Awe is an intuition for the dignity of things, a realization that things not only are what they are but also stand, however remotely, for something supreme. Awe is a sense for the transcendence, for the reference everywhere to mystery beyond all things. It enables us to perceive in the world intimation of the divine ... to sense the ultimate in the common and the simple; to feel in the rush of the passing the stillness of the eternal. What we cannot comprehend by analysis, we become aware of in awe.[23]

Another way for me to visualize and comprehend the concept of quiet in action is the Hindu concept of *detachment from the outcome*. This is the essence of the teaching of the Bhagavad Gita, one of the most important Hindu texts.[24] Arjuna is about to confront the armies of the person who usurped his father's throne: his cousin.[25] As Arjuna faces the upcoming conflict, Lord Krishna admonishes him to engage in the action with purpose and total dedication but without attachment to the outcome. He needs to join in the battle; his cause is just. He needs to put forth his best for the sake of his family and his loyal troops. Once engaged, he cannot be distracted. But, since the outcome is uncertain, attachment to it just saps energy and limits possibilities, affecting the fluidity of movement necessary to handle the vagaries of the battle:

You should never engage in action for the sake of reward, nor should you yearn for inaction. Perform work in this world, Arjuna, as a man established within himself—without selfish attachments, and alike in success and defeat . . . Those who are motivated only by desire for the fruits of action are miserable, for they are constantly anxious about the results of what they do.[26]

With a wise qualifier from Mahatma Gandhi:

But renunciation of fruit in no way means indifference to the results. In regard to every action one must know the result that is expected to follow, the means thereto, and the capacity for it . . . being thus equipped, [be] without desire for the result and yet wholly engrossed in the due fulfillment of the task before [you].[27]

From the Buddhist tradition, Pema Chodron highlights another deep meaning to nonattachment:

"In Vajrayana Buddhism it is said that wisdom is inherent in emotions. When we struggle against our energy we reject the source of wisdom. Anger without the fixation is none other than clear-seeing wisdom. Pride without fixation is experienced as equanimity. The energy of passion when it's free of grasping is wisdom that sees all angles.[28]

Finally, the Bhagavad Gita adds one more consideration that is highly relevant for the entrepreneur: action may be driven and filled with purpose, but it must be *selfless,* and as such it transcends the person. Arjuna did not seek his personal glory; he wanted only to redress the wrong done to his family. In our entrepreneurial efforts, it is not our personal glory that matters but the success of our mission, the realization of our vision. And in the process we do not hesitate to change direction if it enhances the chance of eventual success. This is the entrepreneur's form of nonattachment to the outcome, of going beyond the self. It is the Arjuna in each of us.

Regards,

Ricardo

8

The Companions
on the Journey

Good companions are essential on the road to success. They balance our shortcomings and reinforce our strengths. To sustain a companionship through successes and difficulties requires trust and self-esteem.

Don't walk in front of me, I may not follow,
Don't walk behind me, I may not lead,
Just walk beside me and be my friend.

ALBERT CAMUS

◊

Selfish acts and crooked intentions
crowd around the heart.
Only a real warrior can
tackle that army.

A warrior needs good weapons
and the best of companionship
with the lovers of mystery, the believers.

Drop your spear and join the caravan
of those who set their course
by a sun that never sets.

There's your holy war!
No other decision meets more resistance.
Some part of you
will twist and try to slide away,
for the sight of the good companions
shames that scaly old ego.

Little snakes that have never
seen a true human being
can grow into some
very mean dragons!

JELALUDDIN RUMI

Dear Entrepreneur:

THE ROOT OF THE WORD COMPANION captures the essence of a deep relationship: it comes from the Latin *companio: com* means "together," and *panio* means "bread," so it is someone with whom you break bread. For me, one such person, Jim Cusumano, my Catalytica co-founder, has been such a companion. Our story spans more than a quarter century, from the time I overheard that fateful conversation between Jim and his lab assistant at Exxon in 1973 until we sold the pharmaceutical business in 2000 and Jim retired. The elements of this relationship provide a valuable template for the type of partnership that makes business leadership more effective and successful.

One of the most important ingredients of our relationship was also the essence of being an entrepreneur: a shared dream so powerful that it defined all actions and behavior. Our shared dream was a bright spotlight throughout our history together. It was a constant reminder of what was important, a source of refreshing renewal when we were disappointed, a source of energy when we were exhausted. And it was a wake-up call when ordinary aggravations threatened us, a steady teacher that this was not about us but about something much larger—namely creating a unique, powerful, scientific group motivated to develop breakthrough catalytic technology for the energy and pharmaceutical industries.

Perhaps mindful of future challenges, we put in place at the very beginning of our business relationship a condition that, although mundane, turned out to be essential: we agreed to equal ownership of the company by the three founders under any circumstances. In this way Jim, my PhD adviser Michel Boudart, and I avoided the temptation to "apportion" ownership on the basis of expected future contributions, an almost impossible task, particularly given Michel's continuing full-time affiliation as a professor at Stanford University. Instead, we accepted that we were all essential and that any differences would average out over the life of the company. Besides, if we were as successful as we intended to be, we would all profit so generously that the differences in ownership would be irrelevant; and, if we were not successful, our shares would not matter anyway. Conscious of discrepancies in our own personal financial resources, we even allowed in-kind contributions of seed capital—all in an effort to maintain ownership parity.

This principle would be tested several times over the years. In the early stages of the company, accommodating the compensation needs and demands of the three of us was most difficult, in particular when Michel insisted on receiving his retainer for opening his very extensive network to the company while Jim and I—working practically 24/7 and starting families—were not sure where our next paycheck would come from. In those stress-filled, uncertain times, the sense of inequality was sometimes deep, especially since the value of Michel's network contribution could be recognized only in hindsight. The inviolability of our ownership share decision allowed us to transcend the resentments and permitted our fundamental mutual respect—and shared dream—to prevail.

Equity parity also permitted us later on to take a very difficult step without losing our special partnership. In the early years, science was a key aspect of our corporate identity. As we moved into the development and manufacturing stage, our strategic needs shifted to major business partnerships and financing efforts, and our top leadership—especially on the board of directors—needed to be adjusted accordingly. I personally asked Michel to step off the board, not a simple task given his profound mentorship role in my life. He graciously agreed, staying on in a scientific advisory capacity instead. I attribute the success of this delicate transition to Michel's extraordinary character, our mutual respect and trust, and the parity foundation of our relationship.

A few years later, my partnership with Jim was tested. The company was growing fast as we entered different markets through several subsidiaries. It became clear that the best allocation of talent would be for me to assume the top position in the company, while Jim focused on the pharmaceutical subsidiary instead of being the senior executive in the parent company. Jim accepted this switch in roles—no small step after having served as CEO of the parent company for a decade. His flexibility was a tribute to our special bond of trust and respect, a bond that transcended the most difficult situations we encountered.

Jim remained chair of the parent company's board, an important corporate function, while operationally he focused on the subsidiary. Under normal circumstances this would have been an awkward situation: as head of a subsidiary, he reported to me; as chair of the board, he was my boss. But because of our unique history this never became an issue. As I observe boards of other companies, however, I find that the relationship between the chair and the CEO is not always clear, leading to inefficiencies, and sometimes the lack of clear roles can even jeopardize a company's future if not addressed in a timely manner.

Jim and I had something that I believe is a key to any good and lasting relationship: we each had the right amount of self-confidence *and* self-esteem. Our self-confidence gave us the ability to shine, both externally and in each other's eyes. Our self-esteem gave us enough inner stability to be receptive to each other's ideas and initiatives, preventing jealousy and defensiveness when one of us happened to shine more than the other. This was the foundation of a deep spiritual link between us that transcended form and appearance, providing the basis for complete trust. It permitted our shared dream to blossom fully. In reflecting on our history, Jim observed: "To be honest, I sometimes fought with my ego throughout our decades together. However, in my moments of truth, I always knew that you were more important to me than the insecurities teasing my ego and certainly that our bigger vision for Catalytica was really what mattered."

It is not a coincidence that the word *company* shares the same roots as the word *companion*.

Regards,

Ricardo

9

The Toughest Moments: Layoffs

Circumstances do arise in business life requiring the drastic action of a major reduction in the size of the company. It is one of the worst nightmares I have encountered in my entrepreneurial life. And the hardest part is that a significant layoff sometimes needs to be implemented suddenly, potentially robbing the affected individuals of dignity and a sense of fairness. As part of our covenant with those we invite to join in the journey, we need to be very sensitive to such a disruptive action and take it only as a last resort.

If one could possess, grasp, and know the other,
it would not be other.

EMMANUEL LEVINAS

◇

A good motivation is what is needed: compassion without dogmatism, without complicated philosophy; just understanding that others are human brothers and sisters and respecting their human rights and dignities. That we humans can help each other is one of our unique human capacities.

TENZIN GYATSO, THE FOURTEENTH DALAI LAMA

Dear Entrepreneur:

ON A QUIET DECEMBER AFTERNOON, I was taking a moment to reflect on where we had come with our little company and the many good things that had happened to us along the way. I was influenced by excitement in our scientific ranks about progress on a number of projects, most recently a project to eliminate a very toxic component in the manufacture of high-octane gasoline.

My phone rang. On the line I heard the voice of one of the richest executives in the country. David Koch and his brother Charles owned the largest private enterprise in the energy and petrochemical field: Koch Industries. They had invested in our company a few years earlier and now represented a major part of our research effort. I had dreams that, with our innovative capability and their commercial might, we would be able to make a profound impact in the petroleum and petrochemical industry. By the time I hung up from David's call, the blood had drained from my face, and I felt faint and sick. He had just informed me that his brother, the Koch CEO, had decided to cut out all technology development, and as a result they were severing their relationship with us.

Not only did this shatter our growth plans, but it also created an instant financial crisis. My concern immediately went to my employees. How could I possibly preserve what we had built together? Some of the very talent that Jim and I had recruited so diligently to form one of the best catalysis research and development teams in the world would have to be fired. Yes, fired! The term itself connotes the magnitude of the task and the potential pain in the lives of the individuals affected.

I barely was able to make it to my car and go home. I cried on my wife's shoulder. When I regained my composure, I set about contacting Jim, who was somewhere on the East Coast, doing what he loved best: talking to potential customers about our great technology. I finally located him late that evening in New York City and gave him the news. Bless his soul, his response was, "Ric, you and I will get on a plane tomorrow, and we will find replacements for the Koch brothers. What we have is good, and others will join us!"

Of course, he was right. We were knocked down, but we were far from knocked out. I regrouped and proceeded to make changes in our executive structure that would allow me to reduce the company with dignity and to preserve as much as possible the jewel that we had built. (I will tell you about these structural changes in my next letter.)

This experience led me to deep reflection about the cycle of hiring and layoffs that has become such a pattern in the business world. I vowed that I would never again allow this to happen to us while I was the CEO. We did have subsequent reductions in our workforce, but they came from selling parts of the company—still not easy changes, but with much greater flexibility than in response to a financial crisis. I have participated in other reduction decisions as a board member in other companies, too, and every time I deeply felt the pain of choosing that course. What helped me was my confidence that it was a last resort and that the CEO would carry out the decision with sensitivity. That confidence illustrates part of my board member "trust packet" deposit in those CEOs.

The biggest issue with layoffs is their abrupt nature, beyond the employee's control. They are very different from the changes often necessary in the ordinary course of a healthy business. I believe that dismissing an employee due to poor performance or job mismatch, for example, can be done with dignity and sensitivity, minimizing personal disruption. More often than not, it is the right move for both parties and leads to a sense of relief. One of my close board colleagues, Ken Coleman, gave me this guidance: "Make the decision in your head, and implement it with your heart." That advice, combining the primary interests of the company with compassion for the employee, has often been my modus operandi.[29]

So how does a CEO-with-a-heart deal with the need for major layoffs? Foremost we executives have a responsibility to minimize the possibility of major layoffs. It is part of our leadership covenant and of our contingency thinking when we plan the future, especially during expansion. When layoffs cannot be avoided, I have always made sure that the severance package the employees received was as generous as possible. I practiced this throughout my career, to the consternation of colleagues who were more worried about fiscal concerns.

Perhaps the most relevant step is to help individual employees plan for this situation, anticipating how to handle everything from informing their spouses to adjusting to a sudden life restructuring. It is important to find ways for individual participants in the company to be more cognizant of the risk of layoffs and to address the downside without destroying enthusiasm for the upside of working for the company. Specifically, I suggest an open dialogue with employees about the forces that could affect the destiny of the company and about alternative ways to survive unforeseen events. Such a discussion may, in fact, lead to important creative thinking that actually prevents the worst from happening, because potential pitfalls are thought through far ahead of time. It also leads to deeper bonding with employees, since they become greater co-creators of the future.

A crucial element of the layoff issue for the rank and file is *suddenness*, since the decisions are made by executives and then implemented very quickly. Rapid action is often driven by disclosure requirements for a public company. The suddenness inevitably makes the affected person feel like a disposable asset, without value or human dignity. To put it in even harsher terms, one moment a person is an integral part of the corporate family, a special member of the group, who is expected to be fully engaged and absorbed. The next moment the employee is given notice! Imagine how it must feel as the bond is suddenly torn asunder with the violence of a samurai sword ending a life.

Here is something I have wanted to do but never had a chance to implement: a forum for employees and management, held once a year, with skilled facilitators, to examine issues such as these: Why are you here? Why does the company exist? What is its core raison d'être? What makes it worthwhile for each of us to spend such a major chunk of our lives with the company? How can this life experience—so large a part of our waking hours—be made most meaningful? How do we feel about layoffs? How can layoffs be prevented? Can we imagine circumstances when layoffs would be justified? If so, how would we like to be treated?

In the end, the Koch experience was an important early education for me. For one thing, in future, we made sure to diversify and cross-train our employees. For another, we improved our agreements so that we could reduce our dependence on third parties. I certainly matured quickly and was able to deal with future issues like layoffs a little better, but those decisions never become easy.

Regards,

Ricardo

10

The Dilemma of Changing Roles

Mission, not position, is what matters most in a growing entrepreneurial company. Individual self-interest needs to be left outside the door. Open and clear communication of the company's mission helps, ensuring a nimble, dynamic, and efficient organization, regardless of leadership title. Yet there are times when an entrepreneur needs to assert his or her position at the top of the organization to make sure that responsibility and accountability are established and exercised without equivocation.

Yield and overcome;
Bend and be straight;
Empty and be full;
Wear out and be new;
Have little and gain;
Have much and be confused.

Therefore the wise embrace the one
And set an example to all.
Not putting on a display,
They shine forth.
Not justifying themselves,
They are distinguished.
Not boasting,
They receive recognition.
Not bragging,
They never falter.
They do not quarrel,
So no one quarrels with them.
Therefore the ancients say, "Yield and overcome."
Is that an empty saying?
Be really whole,
And all things will come to you.

LAO TSU

Dear Entrepreneur:

ONCE, AS WE WERE DRIVING TO work in the early days of our company, Jim turned to me in the true spirit of our "executive duo" and asked: "Who do you think should be president, you or I?" My answer was immediate: "You!" He had had a higher position at Exxon and was much more technologically experienced than I, so it seemed obvious that he should have the top title. Besides, I felt as much a critical part of the company, irrespective of title. I continued to be comfortable with the arrangement, even as I increasingly drove the major management aspects of the business, doing in effect the tasks of the CEO. We both tackled the job that needed to be done, conscious of our respective strengths and weaknesses, and we communicated often to avoid any duplication.

The rest of the company employees saw our spirit of cooperation and involvement at the top—they even called it the "Jim and Ric Show"—and were comfortable with a flexible organization. We remained true to a very important requirement of early-stage entrepreneurial companies: *what matters most is mission, not position.*[30] This precept worked well as long as we maintained continuous and effective communication throughout the company. We provided financial and technical updates periodically and talked frequently about how the specific responsibilities of employees related to the overall company strategy, seeking clarity of roles and expectations.

This approach served us very well for many years, even as we grew in size and complexity, allowing us to be nimble and to deploy our limited resources effectively. Then, a couple of events occurred that changed this flexible arrangement, at least at the top. Suddenly, title and position became issues.

The first event occurred in the early 1980s. As a company, we were blessed by a great gift of timing: one of our very active academic collaborators, Henry Taube, received the 1983 Nobel Prize in Chemistry while working with us. This significantly bolstered investor confidence in the caliber of our technical team. It did not, however, change another concern they had: uncertainty about our executive management experience. I learned this while attending a large Harvard Business School event honoring Tommy Davis just as his Mayfield Fund was about to make a second investment in our company. Tommy had a well-earned reputation for being a farsighted and fair venture capitalist—a very rare combination. When he saw me, he put his arm around me and ushered me outside for a long walk (although he was being honored, he did not hesitate to "disappear" for a walk— vintage Tommy). In a caring but firm voice he said, "Ric, we have a big problem ... you do not have enough gray hairs for the amount of money that we are raising." Translation: if you want the money, you and Jim need to step down from the top positions and hire a CEO from outside the company.

This was certainly not the message I wanted to hear, but at least it implied that the money was available. After some serious reflection, Jim and I realized that we had to accept this "request" if we wanted to give our dream a chance. We figured that we might as well embrace the situation and make the best of it: find a mentor, and go to the equivalent of our own business school while doing something we felt passionate about. As a result Dick Fleming, a highly experienced executive, joined our company as CEO to help us navigate this new phase in our growth.

The second event that shook my flexible management attitude was that fateful call from David Koch. In one stroke, one of the largest private companies in the United States ($10 billion in revenues at the time, now nearing $100 billion) was telling our little company to "forget it." The organization that we had seen as our commercialization partner suddenly had disappeared. With that phone call we lost 50 percent of our revenue and a key element of our business strategy. It was clear to me that we had to reduce our company size significantly. It was also clear that I, as founder, had to handle this difficult moment, even though someone else—Dick Fleming—was the CEO. I had been personally involved in attracting every one of the employees, and now I had to face my covenant with them. I had to look each of them in the eyes and tell them that we could not survive with the current staffing, that we had to shrink the company.

I also knew that I could not take on this task unless I

had full responsibility for the company. This was the tipping point for me: position mattered. I could not accomplish my mission without total authority to handle matters in a manner consistent with my values and my sense of fairness. I had to become the CEO. Only then could I ensure that necessary steps were taken to preserve the dignity of those who were asked to leave and to handle with sensitivity the feelings and needs of those who stayed. The process had to be done my way. The board responded, and I was named CEO. Dick, true to his maturity and wisdom, embraced the change and continued to be an important board member for the next years of our critical and exciting growth.

I have often been asked if facing Dick and approaching the change of positions was difficult for me. The answer is very much in line with my discussion of discernment in Letter 7. I knew in my deepest self that this was not only a must for me but also the right step for the company. There was no question. It was not an intellectual matter. I had total conviction, and this authenticity made my conversation with Dick very easy. We immediately turned to the necessary actions together and weathered the tumultuous storm.

Regards,

Ricardo

11

Paradoxical Yet Key Support:
The Board of Directors

A board allows the company to have unparalleled and sophisticated expertise, with individuals who have lived the business-building process and can help navigate the road to success. To maximize the board's effectiveness, an entrepreneur needs to learn to discern between seeing board members as guiding colleagues and seeing them as "the boss."

Beware of the differences that blind us to
the unity that binds us.

HUSTON SMITH

Dear Entrepreneur:

Of ALL THE MANY RELATIONSHIPS
I have built during my business career, the most important
and difficult one has been with my board of directors. I have
always regarded the board as among my most important
resources, offering the company a unique opportunity to
attract the best and most experienced talent to help build the
business. Yet I was also aware that board members played a
dual role: experienced guides and ultimate decision makers.
The board is both teacher and boss.

We entrepreneurs frequently come to our companies with
no board experience. If anything, we attach a mystique to the
board: it's a decision-making body that holds the ultimate
power in the organization. Our "boss" is a group of people—
a new experience for most of us. To make our interactions
even more complex, while we report to the board members,
they depend on us for information, context, and at times
inspiration. Meanwhile, the infrequent board meetings—
typically months apart—require intense preparation and
often frustrating hand-holding.

I had the luxury of "growing into" the subtleties of board
management and leadership, having participated in building
the boards of the companies I co-founded. Early on, I became
aware of how critical it was to keep board members informed
between meetings, ensuring that they could immerse them-

selves in company issues efficiently and expediently. I also learned to focus meeting content to allow enough time for discussion and debate, not just conveyance of information. Even so, for many years I was nervous and tense at board meeting time. I will never forget how my daughter Tammy, who was four years old when we started Catalytica, used to tap me gently on my behind, saying, "It's OK, Daddy. We know you are tense. You must have a board meeting coming up." I was obviously creating enough turmoil around the house to be noticeable even to this small child. Over the years I overcame much of the anxiety, welcoming board meetings as wonderful opportunities to share exciting developments and especially to tap this expert resource for solutions to difficult problems.

I found it very important to have a large enough board so that no single voice dominated. I welcomed strong, accomplished executives, but I also wanted balance—of expertise and personality. Respect among board members was important, so even the quietest voice was sought and heard. And it was essential to build a sense of teamwork, not easy with a group that met only periodically.

To accomplish this I had to realize that I was a full member of the board, with just as much right to be at the table as the most prominent of the other board members. There was no room to feel subservient or intimidated, as those attitudes would seriously jeopardize my ability to be an effective leader. And while another person was chair of the board, titular chief of the group and thus my "boss," I had to remind myself that I was the driving force and heart of the organization and the key architect of its future. The board expected this.

I therefore encourage you to view your board as one of the most valuable teams in your organization. If you manage it well, you will not only derive enormous benefit but also make your life much easier as you reach critical crossroads in the growth of the company. Remember that board members depend on you and are continuously depositing trust packets as they follow your leadership of the organization.[31]

Regards,

Ricardo

12

The Joy of the Entrepreneurial Journey

Few experiences rival the excitement and fulfillment of building a company, and the greatest personal reward comes from touching individual lives while making a difference in society.

The future enters into us, in order to transform
itself in us, long before it happens.

RAINER MARIA RILKE

◊

If I am not for myself, who will be for me?
And if I am for myself alone, what am I?
And if not now, when?

HILLEL THE ELDER

◊

This is the true joy in life: Being used for a purpose recognized
by yourself as a mighty one, being a force of nature instead of
a feverish, selfish little clod of ailments and grievances, com-
plaining that the world will not devote itself to making you
happy. I am of the opinion that my life belongs to the whole
community and as long as I live, it is my privilege to do for it
what I can. It is a sort of splendid torch which I have got hold
of for the moment and I want to make it burn as brightly as
possible before handing it on to future generations.

GEORGE BERNARD SHAW

Dear Entrepreneur:

WHEN YOU READ ABOUT A distinguished person receiving the key to the city from the mayor, have you ever wondered whether it is a real key and whether there is actually a door that it opens (perhaps a special treasure chamber in City Hall)? This medieval concept, implying a walled city, knights, and moats, was always strange to me—until I experienced it personally.

The year was 1997. We had expanded Catalytica Pharmaceuticals by acquiring a 600-acre manufacturing complex in Greenville, North Carolina. The facility had been in a state of uncertainty for several years, on the list for closure or divestiture as a result of a mega-merger of the pharmaceutical giants Glaxo and Borroughs Wellcome. Closure would have created a significant disruption in the community. Our action ensured the continued operation—and anticipated prosperity—of one of the major employers in town. As a result, we were welcomed with open arms by the city, which put on a special celebration hosted by the mayor. Of course, the key was not real, and no, there was no actual door. But the symbolic gesture was a way for a town to express appreciation for special contributions to the community.

The Greenville ceremony represented for us a wonderful confirmation that we were doing something worthwhile, that our actions meant something to others, that we were making an impact. The community's acknowledgment was a very needed and welcome tonic on our entrepreneurial journey, especially given the odds we had overcome to get there.

At the ceremony, when it was Jim's turn to speak, he leaned over and whispered to me an apology for what he was about to do. I braced myself, as he got up and began to sing "The Impossible Dream" from *Man of La Mancha*. The chairman of the board (and I am not talking here about Frank Sinatra) was singing in lieu of making a grandiose speech! He was doing this at a gathering of city officials, invited guests, and almost 2,000 employees. Such a gesture was unheard of in the twenty-five-year history of this facility, formerly a part of one of the largest pharmaceutical companies in the world. The standing ovation that followed said it all. (I should mention that this was not as bizarre as it sounds. When Jim was sixteen, he and his band, The Royal Teens, had made a record that had sold a million copies.)

Later, in a more private gathering, the senior negotiator from Glaxo expressed the same sentiment of hope and optimism as he handed me a copy of the children's story *The Little Engine That Could*.[32] We had indeed succeeded against all odds. For many years after that, the seller of the facility became one of our major customers, and we continued a close involvement with the local and state leadership. The governor of North Carolina eventually invited us to dine with him privately to discuss how to attract more entrepreneurial companies to his state.

For me the real satisfaction and reward of my career came from the individuals I touched directly and personally. The employee who expressed her appreciation for the environment of creativity and cooperation that we fostered in our company, confirming her choice to join us rather than one of the larger companies. The inventor who was welcomed by a management team that recognized the challenges of breakthroughs and showed the necessary patience. The seasoned executive who agreed to serve on our board—and even consulted us on issues he faced in his own company. And on a lighter but no less important note, the employees who, having met at our company, invited us to celebrate their wedding.[33]

We also had the satisfaction of knowing that we were making a difference to society. For example, early in our business we solved a key manufacturing problem in the production of the artificial sweetener Aspartame a few months before it was to be launched by Monsanto. Later, our pharmaceutical company developed part of the synthesis for making Arisept, one of the best-known Alzheimer's drugs. Our Greenville plant became the world manufacturer of the AIDS treatment drug AZT for Glaxo Wellcome as well as the North and South America producer of Zantac 75. And at our Catalytica Energy company in Santa Clara, California, we created the first commercial turbine built with our own catalytic combustor. In the demonstration ceremony at Silicon Valley Power, our invited guests looked at the emission gauges and thought the turbine was not running, since it operated very quietly and produced no measurable pollutants. In fact, we were running at full capacity and delivering clean electrons to the city—electrons produced with our invention.

All this work was based on our mission to develop more effective and environmentally sound manufacturing. It was essential to have such a deeply rooted mission—one that transcended the financial benefits of growth and connected us to a greater purpose. This mission shaped and energized our dream and catalyzed the urge to convert the dream to reality, to share it with others, and to persevere regardless of the obstacles.

Three images have been with me throughout most of my entrepreneurial career. The first is the eighth verse of the ancient Chinese classic, the *Tao Te Ching*:

> *In dwelling, be close to the land.*
> *In meditation, go deep in the heart.*
> *In dealing with others, be gentle and kind.*
> *In speech, be true.*
> *In ruling, be just.*
> *In business, be competent.*
> *In action, watch the timing.*[34]

The second image is a cartoon that shows a stork about to swallow a frog, except that the frog has managed to put his hands around the stork's neck and keep it from swallowing. The caption is "Never, never, never give up"—reminiscent of Winston Churchill's famous exhortation, "Never give in. Never, never, never, never—in nothing, great or small, large or petty—never give in, except to convictions of honour and good sense. Never yield to force. Never yield to the apparently overwhelming might of the enemy."[35]

The third is another cartoon, which appeared in the *New Yorker* in the 1970s. It shows a bearded and robed beggar on a New York street corner with a placard that reads, "Happiness is a positive cash flow."

So, dear entrepreneur, remember that no matter how difficult the road gets, and it surely will be difficult at times, this is a worthwhile journey. Stay true to your inner source, your conviction that your dream is worth bringing to others. Enjoy the dance, and never hesitate to let your unbounded enthusiasm come through. When you invite others to join you in the journey, remember the covenant you enter into with them and the trust packets they are depositing with you. Remain open to those special companions who balance your shortcomings and expand your capabilities. And most important, take time to be quiet, to meditate, and always to keep in touch with your humanity.

I hope I have given you some valuable insights into the journey ahead, principles that articulate ways to make your actions more effective—and ultimately make the journey more meaningful and fun.

In business, watch the timing. Never, ever, give up. Keep the cash flow positive.

Warmly,

Ricardo

$\mathcal{A}$CKNOWLEDGMENTS

This book would not exist, nor, for that matter, would my entrepreneurial career, without the many people who have supported
me over the years. Foremost are my two Catalytica co-founders,
Michel Boudart and Jim Cusumano. I thank Professor Boudart
for his mentorship and guidance and Jim for his long and deep
friendship and his ability to always put our shared dream ahead
of his personal desires and priorities.

There is no excellent company without excellent people, and I
thank each of those who participated in the Catalytica adventure
for making it possible. Bob Garten and Ralph Dalla Betta deserve
special thanks for establishing the rigorous scientific standards
that formed the basis for our discoveries and our reputation as well
as for being early believers in our dream. As the company moved
into manufacturing, our biggest step, acquisition of the Greenville,
North Carolina, manufacturing site, would not have been possible
without Gabe Cipau, who was instrumental in helping us run
that very complex and sophisticated pharmaceutical operation.
Big thanks go to Larry Briscoe, who provided invaluable insight
and skill in our financing efforts, Jackie Cossman, who guided
us through the challenges of a fast-growing public investor base,
and Larry Sonsini, who provided legal counsel and was always
there when I needed him for business wisdom and guidance. The
enterprise and I were also blessed with an extraordinary group of
board members, twenty over three decades and four companies.
We could never have succeeded without them, I was honored to
serve with each one, and I consider them close companions and
mentors. I thank them for all their efforts and dedication.

I thank author and friend Glenda Burgess Grunzweig for her
encouragement and guidance in the writing of this book. She
introduced me to my editor, Alev Croutier, a wonderful teacher

and mentor, who in turn introduced me to Zipporah Collins, who ensured that production stayed on schedule.

I sent early drafts of the manuscript to a number of colleagues for review and critique: Jim Cusumano, Martin McGlynn, Glenda Burgess Grunzweig, André Delbecq, Marc Gunther, and Johanne Bouchard. Their input was invaluable and resulted in revisions and additions. I also thank Ken Coleman for his comments and suggestions, and Jim Koch, Gib Meyers, Barry Posner, Father Richard Rohr, Larry Sonsini, and Bob Worsley for reading the final manuscript.

Finally, I give my greatest thanks to my wife, Noella, who reviewed multiple drafts of the book. She has been my close companion in all my adventures, and I can't imagine how I would have survived the many challenges of my entrepreneurial journey without her as my anchor and support.

Notes

1 Glenda Burgess, *The Geography of Love: A Memoir* (New York: Broadway Books, 2008), 6.

2 Howard Gardner with Emma Laskin, *Leading Minds: An Anatomy of Leadership* (New York: Basic Books, 1995).

3 Chungliang Al Huang and Jerry Lynch, *Mentoring: The Tao of Giving and Receiving Wisdom* (San Francisco: HarperCollins, 1995), 5.

4 I cannot overemphasize the importance of good board members in defining and enabling the future of a company. In Letter 11 I talk about the challenges and opportunities in a leader's relationship with the board. While it takes active management and finesse to deal with the board, good board relations pay critical dividends. I saw this in Ernie Mario's role in the Glaxo deal. It was less a matter of direct action and more that his support had implications for our reputation and his guidance helped us navigate the complex small company–large company interface and negotiation.

5 I became most keenly aware of the covenant issue when a CEO I had hired resigned after two and a half years on the job at a crucial junction for the company. He was attracted to a "better opportunity," catching me totally by surprise. I was chair of the board at the time. What had I missed when I hired him? While he came with a superb reputation as manager, I never recognized that he had no sense of the responsibility an entrepreneurial leader carries, no sense of the *covenant*. When I pointed out to him that he was leaving the company in the lurch, he just said, "Well, the company still has you, so what is the problem?" He did not understand the fabric he had created or the consequences of its rupture. There is another dimension worth noting. When I want to replace an executive, I go out of my way to treat the departing

person well, providing ample time (sometimes months) for the executive to find another job. When a CEO quits for a "better offer," the company is lucky to get three weeks' notice. I call this the *asymmetry of the covenant.*

6 Tommy Davis formed one of the first Silicon Valley venture firms in 1961 with Arthur Rock. Their company invested in ventures that were hugely successful, including Teledyne, Apple Computer, and Intel. In 1969 Tommy formed the Mayfield Fund, which led investments in Catalytica in 1982 and 1984.

7 The capacity of the entrepreneur to create a wake—which is often part of the entrepreneur's magnetic personality—has a downside that needs to be watched. Our "aura" may, in a nonverbal way, give our statements an emphasis or finality beyond our intention. This happens primarily in interactions with employees. While we may be making a simple observation, they may receive our words with much greater force than we would like or want.

8 While I learned to value colleagues with a natural inclination to look for issues and problems in any situation, I always expected them to put as much energy into thinking of ways around these hurdles as into identifying them.

9 I speak more about meditation in Letter 6.

10 Rodger Kamenetz, *Jew in the Lotus: A Poet's Rediscovery of Jewish Identity in Buddhist India* (New York: HarperCollins, 1995), and *Stalking Elijah: Adventures with Today's Jewish Mystics* (New York: HarperCollins, 1997).

11 Xonon (no-NOx spelled backward) was Catalytica's trademark for the discovery of a catalyst that was able to burn fuel without creating any oxides of nitrogen (chemical symbol

NOx.) These oxides are the cause of brown smog in our cities and are one of the very toxic components of air pollution created by automobiles and fossil fuel power plants.

12 André L. Delbecq, "Spirituality for Business Leadership: Reporting on a Pilot Course for MBAs and CEOs," *Journal of Management Inquiry* 9 (2000): 117–128.

13 Ricardo B. Levy, "My Experience as Participant in the Course on Spirituality for Executive Leadership," *Journal of Management Inquiry* 9 (2000): 129–131.

14 Pema Chodron, *The Places That Scare You: A Guide to Fearlessness in Difficult Times* (Boston: Shambhala, 2001), 83.

15 Alan Lew, *Be Still and Get Going: A Jewish Meditation Practice for Real Life* (New York: Little, Brown, 2005), 191.

16 For my mantra I use the word *shema*, which in Hebrew means "listen" or "hear." It is the beginning of the prayer from Deuteronomy 6:4: *Shema Yisrael, Adonai Elohaynu, Adonai Echad* (Hear, O Israel, the Lord is our God, the Lord is One). Sometimes I spontaneously move to another mantra, the four Hebrew letters representing the sacred name of the Lord in the Jewish tradition: YHVH. As I say it, I mentally move through my body, attaching meaning to each letter, in line with the practice of the Jewish mystics. To the letter V (*vav*) I attach the wonderful balancing manifestations of the divine: love balanced by judgment; power balanced by humility. When I say the second H (*heh*), I think of Shekhinah, the earth.

17 I am often asked about resources for learning meditation. My advice is to go to several sources and see what speaks to you most directly and intimately. Here are some of the sources that inspired me: The centering prayer approach described by Father Thomas Keating in *Open Mind, Open Heart* (New

York: Continuum, 1999) and many of the writings of Father
Laurence Freeman, such as *Jesus: The Teacher Within* (New
York: Continuum, 2001). The guided meditations in Rabbi
Arthur Green's *Ehyeh: A Kabbalah for Tomorrow* (Wood-
stock, VT: Jewish Lights, 2003), especially pages 44 and 82.
The use of the *shivity* in Rabbi Zalman Schachter-Shalomi's
Jewish Renewal Teachings, *Paradigm Shift*, ed. Ellen Singer
(Lanham, MD: Jason Aronson Publishers, 1993), 165–168.
Starting my meditation with a spiritual reading as described
by Eknath Easwaran in *Passage Meditation*, 3rd ed. (Tomales,
CA: Nilgiri Press, 2008), and his wonderful compendium of
inspirational passages, *Timeless Wisdom* (Tomales, CA: Nil-
giri Press, 2008). Finally, some of the prayer practices of the
Muslim tradition described in Coleman Barks and Michael
Green's book *The Illuminated Prayer* (New York: Ballantine,
2000), 115–130.

18 Part of the practice of meditation is recognizing the power of
silence. Just as Rabbi Lew reminded us of the value of deep
breath, taking some time to be quiet before action helps us
all gain composure, perspective, and focus. I saw the value of
this in the most unlikely place: at board meetings. I initiated a
practice in all the meetings of Catalytica's board of directors:
a few minutes of silence before we started our sessions. It
allowed all of us to leave our individual external preoccupa-
tions behind and focus on the business at hand. Considering
the composition of our board—major executives from large
multinational corporations—it was especially rewarding to
see how well received this practice became. In fact, at one
meeting when we had a long agenda and I kept the initial
silence period short, some board members grumbled that I
had not allowed enough time for it.

19 Werner Heisenberg, quoted by Gino Segre in *Faust in Copen-hagen* (New York: Penguin Books, 2007), 150.

20 Julian Gresser, *Piloting through Chaos: Wise Leadership, Effective Negotiation for the 21st Century* (Sausalito, CA: Five Rings Press, 1996), 64, quoting John Keats, Letter to his brothers George and Thomas Keats, December 21, 1817.

21 The Jesuit tradition points to the need to be in the unknown as a requirement for good discernment. In the Ignatian Spiritual Exercises, a complex thirty-step process that every Jesuit priest is required to undergo when he joins the order, the practitioner learns to become very sensitive to inner signals of comfort (consolation) or unease (desolation), which become the messengers that guide the spiritual discernment process. To reach that state requires practice in inner silence as well as deep self-knowledge and self-acceptance. See John J. English, *Spiritual Freedom: From an Experience of the Ignatian Exercises to the Art of Spiritual Guidance*, 2nd rev. ed. (Chicago: Loyola Press, 1995).

22 Hung Ying-ming, "Ts'ai-ken T'an," *Parabola* 30, no. 2 (Summer 2005): 1.

23 Abraham Joshua Heschel, *I Asked for Wonder* (New York: Crossroads, 2001), 3.

24 *The Bhagavad Gita*, 2nd ed., trans. Eknath Easwaran, Classics of Indian Spirituality Series (Tomales, CA: Blue Mountain Center of Meditation, 2007).

25 Facing his relatives and some of his former teachers, Arjuna struggles with the rightness of the battle he is about to enter and pursues a dialogue with his charioteer, who is the Lord Krishna in disguise. It is hard to imagine a more gripping situation. In a fight with your own kin it is impossible to "depersonalize" the enemy.

26 *The Bhagavad Gita*, 66.

27 Mahatma Gandhi, quoted in the Preface to Eknath Easwaran's edition of *The Bhagavad Gita*, xl.

28 Pema Chodron, *The Places That Scare You: A Guide to Fearlessness in Difficult Times* (Boston: Shambhala, 2001), 29.

29 Ken Coleman was one of the key executives who implemented and fostered the "HP way" under Bill Hewlett and David Packard. See David Packard, *The HP Way: How Bill Hewlett and I Built Our Company* (New York: HarperCollins, 1996).

30 I borrowed this expression from André Delbecq.

31 Lessons to keep in mind with boards: (1) Always build a board that is bigger than you need. (2) Strongly opinionated executives with a proven track record are good to have—as long as you have several, and they respect one another. Their opinions will balance and optimize the outcome. The critical factor is not their individual strengths but the *composite* of their inputs and wisdom. (3) Even the board member who at times seems most difficult and "marginal" makes a contribution at the right time. (4) Management of the board requires a strong CEO and a strong chair. Good teamwork between CEO and chair is critical. (5) Follow the key "rule of 3" to attract a board member: First, get the person excited about the vision; second, assure the candidate that association with your company will never tarnish his or her reputation (this assurance is best done by pointing to who else has agreed to serve); and third, be super-respectful of board members' time. (6) Do not shy away from internal referrals when looking for new board members. High quality attracts high quality.

32 Watty Piper, *The Little Engine That Could* (New York: Platt and Munk, Publishers, 1930).

33 This all literally "came home" to me recently. Well over a

decade ago, someone in the company started a Catalytica "Yahoo Group" as an informal link among company members. It had not been used much since the company was sold. However, in the fall of 2009 a past employee sent a note through this social network link requesting help because her husband had been out of work for over a year and things were getting very tight. The response was overwhelming, with multiple concrete offers of job assistance. This prompted me to invite the few Catalytica alumni I thought still resided in my area to come to dinner in early December at our home. Because headquarters for the various companies that developed from Catalytica had moved to other parts of the country as we sold or merged them, my wife and I thought we would have a quiet dinner for twenty or so. Before we knew it, the positive RSVPs neared seventy, including several who decided to travel long distances to come. While pushing to an extreme the capacity of our modest home, we managed. The intensity of the connection between the attendees, some of whom had not seen one another for more than two decades, was heartwarming, testimony to the bond that our company had created. As one of the attendees commented during the evening, it was a tribute to the special culture that we had built, a culture that started at the top. The best news was that, thanks to one of the Yahoo Group responses, the out-of-work husband had received a job offer a few weeks before.

34 Lao Tsu, "The Way of Water," *Tao Te Ching: A New Translation by Gia-Fu Feng and Jane English*, Verse 8 (New York: Vintage, Random House, 1972). Reprinted by permission.

35 Winston Churchill, speech, October 29, 1941, to the boys at Harrow School; reprinted at www.school-for-champions .com/speeches/churchill_never_give_in.htm.

$\mathscr{A}$BOUT QUOTED AUTHORS

SAINT THOMAS AQUINAS (circa 1225–1274) Catholic thinker and theologian, author of the *Summa Theologica*.

SAINT AUGUSTINE (354–430) Also known as Augustine of Hippo; Catholic theologian and writer who played a major part in the development of Christian thought.

ALBERT CAMUS (1913–1960) French author and existential philosopher; awarded the Nobel Prize in Literature in 1957.

PEMA CHODRON (1936–) Born in New York, a contemporary English-language Tibetan Buddhist teacher and author.

DEEPAK CHOPRA (1946–) Indian-born, American-trained physician who lectures and writes on alternative medicine and mind–body well-being.

WINSTON CHURCHILL (1874–1965) British prime minister, political and military leader, historian, and writer; awarded the Nobel Prize in Literature in 1953.

SAINT FRANCIS DE SALES (1567–1622) French Catholic theologian, revered for his practical teachings on spiritual formation and devotion.

MAHATMA GANDHI (1869–1948) Given name Mohandas; Indian spiritual and political leader who preached and practiced nonviolence and civil disobedience.

HOWARD GARDNER (1943–) Professor of Cognition and Education at Harvard University and proponent of the theory of multiple intelligences.

JOHANN WOLFGANG VON GOETHE (1749–1832) German poet, novelist, dramatist, and philosopher.

JULIAN GRESSER (1943–) American attorney and author specializing in environmental and international law and business strategy.

TENZIN GYATSO, the Fourteenth Dalai Lama (1935–) Tibetan Buddhist spiritual leader.

WERNER HEISENBERG (1901–1976) German theoretical physicist who played a major role in the development of quantum theory.

RABBI ABRAHAM JOSHUA HESCHEL (1907–1972) Jewish mystical thinker and writer. His most significant thoughts are compiled in his book *I Asked for Wonder: A Spiritual Anthology*, ed. Samuel H. Dresner (New York: Crossroad Publishing Co., 1983).

HILLEL THE ELDER (circa 110 BCE–10 CE) Jewish teacher and commentator, who was born in Babylon and lived in Jerusalem at the time of King Herod. When asked to summarize the essence of Judaism, his famous answer was, "What is hateful to thee, do not unto thy fellow man: this is the whole Law; the rest is mere commentary." The Mishnah, Shabbat 31a.

CHUNGLIANG AL HUANG (1937–) Tai Chi (Tai Ji) teacher and master, founder of the Living Tao Foundation in Gold Beach, OR, and author and public speaker on spiritual philosophy.

HUNG YING-MING (late 1500s) Chinese author during the end of the Ming Dynasty, known for his book *Ts'ai-ken T'an* (or *Saikontan*) combining Taoist, Confucian, and Buddhist philosophies.

RODGER KAMENETZ (1950–) Jewish author and poet, on the faculty of Louisiana State University, who participated in a 1990 historic meeting between Jewish leaders and the Dalai Lama in Tibet, recorded in his book *The Jew in the Lotus: A Poet's Rediscovery of Jewish Identity in Buddhist India* (New York: HarperCollins, 1995).

LAO TSU (circa 604–531 BCE) Chinese sage and author of the *Tao Te Ching*, one of the foundations of Taoism.

EMMANUEL LEVINAS (1906–1995) Lithuanian-born French philosopher and Talmudic scholar, known for his emphasis

on deeply caring for other human beings as the source of
goodness.

RABBI ALAN LEW (1944–2009) Teacher of Jewish spirituality
and Zen Buddhist meditation.

JOHN MILTON (1608–1674) English poet, author of *Paradise
Lost*.

W. H. MURRAY (1913–1996) Full name William Hutchison Murray; Scottish mountaineer and writer, who drafted his book
Mountaineering in Scotland while a prisoner of the Germans
during World War II.

RAINER MARIE RILKE (1875–1926) Prague-born Bohemian
author of poetry and lyric prose.

JELALUDDIN RUMI (1207–1273) Sufi mystic and Persian spiritual
poet and thinker.

GEORGE BERNARD SHAW (1856–1950) Dublin-born playwright,
winner of the Nobel Prize in Literature in 1925.

HUSTON SMITH (1919–) Born in China to American missionary
parents, a philosopher and historian of world religions.

ECKHART TOLLE (1948–) German-born spiritual teacher, public
speaker, and author.

$\mathcal{E}$PIGRAPH SOURCES

LETTER 1

"Changing How We Age: Veronica Hay Interviews Deepak Chopra, M.D.," http://www.facebook.com/topic.php?uid=1080 6621169&topic=8434. The concepts are elaborated upon in "The Law of 'Dharma' or Purpose in Life," chapter 7 of Chopra's book *The Seven Spiritual Laws of Success: A Practical Guide to the Fulfillment of Your Dreams* (Novato, CA: New World Library, 1994), which is reproduced at http://www.scribd.com/doc/19873/The-Seven-Spiritual-Laws-Of-Success and discussed at http://deepakchopra.com/category/interact-blog/7-spiritual-laws/.

LETTER 2

W. H. Murray, *The Scottish Himalayan Expedition* (London: J. M. Dent & Sons, 1951). The quoted couplet by Johann Wolfgang von Goethe is from his play *Faust*, lines 214–230, loosely translated by John Anster in 1835.

LETTER 3

Eckhart Tolle, *A New Earth: Awakening to Your Life's Purpose* (New York: Penguin, 2006), 274.

LETTER 6

The Bhagavad Gita (Song of the Blessed Lord), a section of *The Mahabharata*, one of the two sacred Hindu epics of ancient India.

LETTER 7

Deepak Chopra, "The Law of Detachment," chapter 6 of *The Seven Spiritual Laws of Success: A Practical Guide to the Fulfillment of Your Dreams* (Novato, CA: New World Library, 1994), which is reproduced at http://www.scribd.com/doc/19873/The-Seven-Spiritual-Laws-Of-Success and featured at http://deepakchopra.com/2008/10/6-the-law-of-detachment/.

LETTER 8

Jelaluddin Rumi, *One Song: A New Illuminated Rumi*, ed. Michael Green (Philadelphia: Running Press, 2005).

LETTER 9

Emmanuel Levinas, *The Levinas Reader*, ed. Sean Hand, Blackwell Readers series (Hoboken, NJ: Wiley-Blackwell, 2001), 51, quoted at http://www.bactroid.net/~fuzzcat/nine_finger_monarchy/quotes.html.

Tensin Gyatso, the Fourteenth Dalai Lama, quoted at http://www.wisdomquotes.com/cat_compassion.html.

LETTER 10

Lao Tsu, *Tao Te Ching: A New Translation by Gia-Fu Feng and Jane English*, Verse 22 (New York: Vintage Books, Random House, 1972). Reprinted by permission.

LETTER 11

Huston Smith, *The Way Things Are: Conversations with Huston Smith on the Spiritual Life*, ed. Phil Cousineau (Berkeley and Los Angeles: University of California Press, 2003), 36.

LETTER 12

Rainer Maria Rilke, *Duino Elegies*, trans. J. B. Leishman and Stephen Spender (New York: W. W. Norton, 1969), 1.

Hillel the Elder, quoted in Mishnah Pirkei Avot (Ethics of the

Fathers), 1:14, a Jewish commentary on the Torah (the first five books of the Old Testament).

George Bernard Shaw, "Epistle Dedicatory to Arthur Bingham Walkley," *Man and Superman: A Comedy and a Philosophy* (New York: Classic Books International, 2009), 21.

ABOUT THE AUTHOR

RICARDO B. LEVY is an executive and entrepreneur whose career spans more than three decades of founding and building successful businesses. Born and raised in South America to a European immigrant family, he completed engineering studies in the United States at Stanford and Princeton before returning to South America to run a family business. In 1969 he sold the business and returned to the United States to complete his PhD at Stanford in the field of catalytic chemistry. In 1974, after a number of years in the petroleum and petrochemical industry, he co-founded his first entrepreneurial venture, Catalytica, a research and development firm serving the chemical, pharmaceutical, and energy industries. The firm's discoveries resulted in over one hundred patents and led to the formation of three companies, one of which became, under Levy's leadership, the largest supplier to the pharmaceutical industry in North America. He currently serves on several public and private corporate boards of directors.